KiD CAMPiNG
from
Aaaaiii! to ZIP

Patrick F. McManus

Illustrated by Roy Doty

Lothrop, Lee & Shepard Books   New York

KiD GAMPiNG
from
Aaaaiii! to ZIP

Acknowledgment

My wife, Darlene,
deserves enormous credit
for her comments and criticism,
the spelling and typing,
and the omission
of several dozen bad jokes.

Printed in the United States of America.
First Edition   1 2 3 4 5 6 7 8 9 10

Library of Congress Cataloging in Publication Data

McManus, Patrick F.
  Kid camping from Aaaaiii! to Zip.

  Includes index.
  SUMMARY: Humorous and practical advice on various aspects of camping, presented alphabetically.

  1. Camping—Anecdotes, facetiae, satire—Juvenile literature. [1. Camping] I. Doty, Roy, (date) II. Title.
GV191.7.M28   796.54   79-13152
ISBN 0-688-41910-0
ISBN 0-688-51910-5 lib. bdg.

For my own kid campers:
Kelly,
Shannon,
Peggy,
and Erin

Contents

Introduction

The reason that many men and women camp all their lives may be that they are trying to recapture the fun and joy and excitement of kid camping. It can't be done. Kid camping has only one requirement: being a kid. You can be a girl kid or a boy kid but you must be a kid. Otherwise you cannot know true kid camping.

To a grownup, a backyard at night is only a backyard at night. To a kid, a backyard at night is a vast and mysterious frontier, and sleeping there, a journey into the unknown. No explorer ever returned from an expedition more haggard and more exhausted or with a greater sense of accomplishment than an eight-year-old returning from his or her first night of sleeping out alone in the Great Backyard.

Grownups have no grasp of the distances involved in kid camping. They might suppose that a kid is sleeping out only twenty-five feet from the back door of the house. But to kids, the Sahara Desert, Mount Everest, and the Amazon may lie between them and the back door. Grownup observers may calculate that a kid travels the distance home in exactly two seconds. They don't realize the kid has five years crammed into each of those seconds.

Nor do grownups know anything about kid camp cooking. What is "burnt to a crisp" to an adult is "done" to a kid. An adult's junk foods are a kid's staples. What a mother may think is robbing her refrigerator is thought of by a kid as "living off the land."

9

The sound a grownup identifies as the mournful cry of a night bird may be a kid's non-stop ticket home. Maybe not, though. You can't predict kid campers.

There are spaces, you see, that grownups cannot cross, no matter how much they would like to return to kid camping. But if the grownups were once kid campers, they can always remember how it was. This is what I have attempted to do in writing this book, to remember exactly how it was. I have tried to describe the various aspects of kid camping as I knew them in a distant time and place but which I believe are the same today as they were then. Sleeping out alone for the first time is always sleeping out alone for the first time; it is an experience that will remain the same for all eternity.

Gradually, kid camping becomes grownup camping, which, to my mind, means backpacking. In addition to kid camping basics, therefore, I have also attempted to give you information that will be of use to you in your progress toward backpacking. Backpacking will never be quite as good as kid camping but it's the next best thing.

My research for this book has included personal interviews with my own four daughters, two of whom are still kid campers and two of whom were recently kid campers. I have also interviewed the kid camping sons of a friend of mine, and they have been most helpful in recalling certain details I might otherwise have overlooked. For example, when Jimmy asked me what the first topic in my book was to be, I told him, "Air Mattress."

"Air Mattress?" he said, astounded. "What about *Aaaaiii!?*"

"Gosh," I said, "I'd forgotten all about *Aaaaiii!*"

"And what's the last topic going to be?" Jimmy asked, now more than a little doubtful about my book on kid camping.

"Zip," I said.

"Ah, good," he said. "I'm glad you didn't forget Zip."

"Listen," I told him, "nobody who has experienced Zip ever forgets it!"

A *Aaaaiii!*

This is a sound often heard on kid camping trips. You won't have any trouble recognizing the *Aaaaiii!* sound because it will cause your hair to jump up and stand at attention. If you hear a strange noise and your hair just lies there on your head twitching a bit, then that isn't your true *Aaaaiii!* Almost any noise at night can raise a crop of goose bumps on campers but it takes an *Aaaaiii!* to lift their hair.

Occasionally, your brother or sister or one of the other campers will make the *Aaaaiii!* sound when the presence of a crawly thing is detected in a sleeping bag (see Crawly Things). "*Aaaaiii!*" they will say. "There's a crawly thing in my sleeping bag!" Your hair will still jump up, but as soon as it finds out the sound is coming from only your brother or sister or one of the other campers it will flop back down and relax.

If it turns out that you're the one going *Aaaaiii!*, then that's serious. One time when I was a kid somebody slipped a big, old, cold, clammy frog into my sleeping bag. Just as I was getting comfortably settled in the bag, the frog took it into his head to scramble up onto my leg. It was enough to unloose an *Aaaaiii!* from an alligator, let alone a kid. Still, I was embarrassed. I tried to explain to the other campers that I was trying to raise an echo off the mountain, but since the mountain was four miles away they didn't believe me. All they could do was lie there in their sleeping bags cackling like a flock of hens. Then the echo of my *Aaaaiii!* arrived

in camp and it was still strong enough to raise a few hairs. That put an end to the cackling. The point is, it's a good idea to have a sensible explanation prepared for those occasions in which you are startled into releasing an *Aaaaiii!* "I was just practicing my Tarzan yell" is a good one.

The real hair-straighteners are the *Aaaaiii*!s that come drifting out of the woods on a dark night. One time my friends Retch and Henry and I were camped out in a wilderness area sometimes referred to as Fergussens' Wood Lot. The campfire had died down and we were lying in our sleeping bags exchanging a few ghost stories, when suddenly a long, loud, quavering *Aaaaiii!* came drifting out of the shadows. Why, there wasn't a hair on us that couldn't have been used for an ice pick.

After a bit, Henry said, "I think maybe it was only a bird."

"Y-yeah," Retch said. "A five-hundred-pound kid-eating b-bird!"

But Henry was one of those people who always have to think up a common-sense reason for every weird thing that happens. "I got it!" he said. "It was probably your cousin Buck! He sneaked out here and is trying to scare us!"

I thought Henry might be right about my cousin, because it was the sort of mean thing Buck liked to do. The problem was that Retch and I had already shucked off our sleeping bags and wound up our legs. Of course, once your legs are wound up, there is only one thing you can do, and that is to point yourself toward home and let them unwind, which is what we did. Henry said later he had planned on spending the rest of the night out in the wilderness by himself but when Retch and I let our legs unwind we created such a vacuum that he was sucked right along behind us. Retch and I didn't believe him for one moment.

"How come, then, you passed us before we were even halfway home, Henry? Tell me that!" I said.

"Yeah," Retch said, "and you not even out of your sleeping bag yet!"

Henry couldn't think up a single common-sense answer.

I've never heard of *Aaaaiii*!s causing any actual harm, and if nothing else, they contribute a great deal to the overall excitement of camping. On the other hand, they are something I could do without.

Adults

Adults frequently accompany kids on camping trips. These trips can be fun but they are not true kid camping. They are adult camping. The adults decide where to camp, where to pitch the tent, how to build the fire, what to cook for dinner, when to go to bed and so on. The adults try not to decide all these things but they can't help themselves.

Sometimes the adult will say, "All right, Barbara and Ann, you pitch the tent, and Sid, you gather some wood and build us a campfire, and Pete, you cook supper." That would be fine if the adult would then go off and take a nap under a tree, but no, he or she will stand around looking worried, gasping from time to time, murmuring, shuddering and twitching, until the kids are so nervous they can hardly think straight. Eventually, the adult will say something like, "Say, let me give you a hand with that." What he or she means is, "Now I'm going to show you how to do it right."

When I was a kid I used to go on outings with the old woodsman Rancid Crabtree. Rancid would almost always build the campfire himself, but occasionally he would tell me, "Whup us up a fahr." Naturally, I would be pleased that Rancid felt I was capable of building a fire, and I would set happily about the task. He would stand behind me, peering over my shoulder. "Naw," he would say. "Don't do thet. You need more shavings. Let me show you how to whittle shavings fer a fahr. Hold it, them sticks is too big. Use these little sticks. No, don't pile 'em up like thet." Somehow the fire-building always ended with me standing behind Rancid, peering over his shoulder. "Thar," he would say at last, "danged if you didn't build us a purty good fahr."

14

Adults are always saying dumb things to kids on camping trips. "Don't get lost," they will say. "Don't fall in the creek. Don't get stung by a bee." Do you suppose they think the kids are saying to themselves, "Gee, now I think I'll go get lost, fall in the creek, and after that maybe I'll get stung by a bee"?

One nice thing about having adults along on camping trips is that they always know what the *Aaaaiii!* sound is. An *Aaaaiii!* will come drifting out of the woods and a kid will ask, "Gee, what was that?"

The adult will consider the question for a moment and then reply, "That was an *Aaaaiii!*"

If a good loud quavering *Aaaaiii!* doesn't make an adult's hair stand on end like yours, keep in mind that there is a simple explanation for this: he is older, wiser, more experienced in the outdoors, and, most probably, bald.

Finally, never engage in standard kid camping practices when you are with adults. Adults are easily shocked out of their senses by standard kid camping practices. And if that happens, who is going to drive the car home?

Air

Air is very important to campers. The most important kind of air for campers is called "open air." This is the kind of air that camping takes place in. Open air is any air that isn't inside a building. The air in your backyard, for example, is open air and good for camping. The main thing kid campers want to keep in mind about open air is not to have too much of it between them and their house.

Then there's thin air. The higher you go, the thinner the air. When your mother and father start huffing and puffing on a hike, they may explain that they're breathing so hard because the air is thinner now than when they were kids. This is true. I've noticed it myself. Since kids are shorter than adults, they get to breathe the fat air. I'm pretty sure that's how it works.

Adult campers enjoy smelling the air. Perhaps you have noticed that whenever they get out of a car at the beginning of a camping trip, they always say, "Ah, smell that air! Doesn't it smell good!" The reason campers smell the air at the beginning of a camping trip is that after a while, all they'll be able to smell is the other campers. Anyway, I've never heard anybody say, "Ah, smell that air!" at the *end* of a camping trip.

I myself like to smell air on camping trips. You can tell all sorts of things from smelling the air. Once I smelled an argument that had taken place several days before between a coyote and a skunk. It didn't smell all that good, but it was interesting just the same. One of the best things to smell in the open air is the aroma of wild strawberries ripe and hot under a July sun. You can smell rain in the air, too. If the weather has been hot and dry for a long time and suddenly there's a little shower, the rain smells really fresh and good. Once you've tried it, you too will enjoy smelling the rain. Oh, I don't mean you'll get up in the middle of the night and hike halfway across the county just to smell some rain, but if it happens along you'll enjoy smelling it.

Another kind of air you find on grownup camping trips is hot air. The hot air comes from all the stories that are told around a campfire. You know a blast of hot air is coming whenever a grownup camper leans back and says, "Say, did I ever tell you the time . . ." Many's the camping trip I've been warmed all over by this kind of hot air. It's nice. If the day is cold and wet and you can't get a campfire going, you might try starting a story-teller, just to warm you up a bit. But even though storytellers give off plenty of hot air, it's not a good idea to try to roast a marshmallow over one of them. Once a melted marshmallow has dropped in his hair, it's almost impossible to get a storyteller started again. You'd have better luck with a fire.

Air Mattress

Kid campers can get along fine without air mattresses. In the opinion of many experienced campers, air mattresses may even be more bother than they are worth. However, if you find that the ground is unbearably hard, by all means get yourself an air mattress. Inflated properly, it can provide you with a comfortable night's sleep.

Don't waste your money on a cheap, plastic air mattress, because it will puncture the first night out and, with a long sigh, lower your backside, or some other portion of your anatomy, onto the object that did the puncturing. This in turn will cause you to let out the famous *Aaaaiii!* sound and unnerve all the rest of the camp.

The kind of air mattress to buy is one made of either coated nylon or rubberized canvas. Get the three-quarter-length size because it will save weight in your pack and be quicker to inflate. Your lower legs and feet may complain for a while about being cheated, but just ignore them. At your present height, the three-quarter length will probably be full length for you anyway. With a bit of luck, you will grow until it becomes a three-quarter length, and a quality air mattress should last at least until then.

Some air mattresses have a little tube for the air to go in (fine) and also for the air to come out (not so fine). In the morning, it will take what seems like hours to squeeze all the air out through that little tube. You'll be a mile down the trail with the rest of the troops, and still hugging your air mattress to squeeze the air out of it. This can be embarrassing if nothing else. Fortunately, some genius came up with the idea of putting a large plug in air mattresses for the purpose of letting out the air. If you buy an air mattress, get one with a large plug in it. While still lying on the mattress in the morning, you need only remove the plug and all the air rushes out in a single satisfying *whoosh!*

The mistake many beginning campers make with air mattresses is that they inflate them too hard. The proper method for inflating an air mattress is to blow it up, then lie on your side on it and

AIR MATTRESS

release air slowly from the *small* tube until by pressing down hard you can feel the ground with your hip. Then cap the tube. The air mattress will now fit your shape and keep even your lowest parts suspended comfortably a couple of inches off the ground.

Air Mattress Pump

Numerous kinds of pumps are sold for the purpose of inflating air mattresses, but the best inflator I know of is the pink, portable model known as lungs. Lungs will do the job almost as quickly as the store-bought pumps, they don't take up room in your pack or add weight, and every camper already has a pair. Best of all, you almost never forget and leave them at home.

Air Pillow

Even though you decide to do without an air mattress, you may want an air, or inflatable, pillow. A pair of rolled-up pants doesn't make a comfortable headrest. There is only one thing more painful on a camping trip than getting your ear caught in a pants zipper. (I forget what it is at the moment, but you wouldn't want it to happen to you.)

Alarms

Say you and the other campers are in your sleeping bags and starting to get nice and comfortable. The campfire has died down and the last ghost story has been told. You are starting to doze off. Then one of the other campers whispers, "Did you hear something just then?"

That's an alarm.

Nothing can pop a camper's eyes open faster than that kind of whisper, except maybe an *Aaaaiii!* The alarm must be a whisper, though. Suppose somebody asks in a normal voice, "Did you hear something just then?" The other campers will reply "No. Shut up and go to sleep." But if a whisper is used, all the campers lie there quieter than wet moss with their eyelids snapped up and their ears flared out. After a bit, somebody will whisper to the alarmist, "What did it sound like?" The alarmist will now know that he has everybody's attention and will start to feel important. "I don't know," he'll whisper back. "I've never heard anything like it before in my whole life!" Right there the alarmist makes certain there won't be an eye blink in camp for fifteen minutes. Presently, another camper will whisper, *"There!* I heard it too." The first alarmist will hiss back, "You did? What'd it sound like?" And so on, until every last camper thinks he or she has heard the sound. By then, the first alarmist will have become bored with the whole thing and have gone to sleep. After the alarm has run its course among the other campers, they too will go to sleep. Campers recover quickly from alarms, not counting the few days they go about with cramps in their flared ears.

Aluminum Foil

Heavy-duty aluminum foil makes fine temporary pots, pans, ovens and other utensils for camp cooking.

A foil frying pan can be made by bending and tying a green branch into the shape of a tennis racket and covering the rounded end with foil. Also wrap the handle in foil so that it won't catch fire. A similar pan can be made by covering the forked end of a stick with foil.

Pots and pans can be made by folding foil into the shape of a pot or kettle. The seams should be crimped tight and then folded over and crimped again. Roll down the top edge to make the pot stronger and to make it hold its shape better. Foil pots should not be made much larger than cereal bowls, because they usually are not strong enough to hold more than a couple of cupfuls. Foil pans are made about the size of a sheet of notebook paper. Larger ones can be made, but they tend to become limp and floppy. The sides of the pan should be an inch or two high.

Aluminum foil makes good heat reflectors. Here's a way to roast a whole chicken using a foil reflector. A foil pan is placed under the chicken to catch the drippings, which are then used to baste the chicken. The chicken can also be baked using this same setup but wrapping the entire chicken in foil. If the chicken is wrapped completely in foil, it will be more tender and juicy, but won't have the crisp brown skin or the same smoky flavor as a chicken roasted uncovered over the coals. (Also see Cooking: *Roast Chicken.*)

Food can also be cooked in foil packages that are placed directly on the coals. A complete dinner for a camper can be cooked in this way. A typical foil package dinner might include a beef patty, potato slices (cut about as thick as one of your fingers so they won't cook either too fast or too slowly), onion slices, and whole-kernel corn. Or you can try whatever combination of foods you like. The food is arranged on a sheet of foil and salted and peppered to taste; margarine or butter can be dabbed on the potatoes and corn and anything else you think might be improved by it. Fold up the foil over your dinner and double-crimp the ends; fold the top of the foil down and double-crimp it; your foil dinner package should now be tightly sealed. If these directions sound too complicated, just fold up the package anyway you like, only make sure you have a tight seal on all the seams.

The one problem with foil package dinners is that it is hard to tell when your food is cooked. A good rule is to place the package on the coals and let it cook on one side for ten minutes, then turn it over and let it cook on the other side for ten minutes. Your dinner should turn out about right, at least by camp cooking standards. Don't put your foil package dinner in the flames of the fire. I have tried this several times, and my beef patty and potato slices came out looking, and tasting, like dominoes without the white spots. Use a couple of sticks to turn your foil package on the coals and to lift it. Open the package with a knife or stick, and it will cool off much quicker. Don't be eager to grab the package with your fingers. Every time I've seen campers grab their foil package too soon after it's come off the coals, they have produced a fine *Aaaaiii!* and quite often a rather wild little dance to go with it.

Ears of corn wrapped in foil and roasted over coals are delicious. Dab with margarine or butter before sealing foil.

The shiny side of the foil should be placed toward the food, because it reflects more heat than the dull side. If the shiny side

FOIL REFLECTOR OVEN

is out, it will reflect the heat away from your food and dinner will take longer to cook.

Foil can be used to make a reflector oven for cooking biscuits, cowboy coffeecake, and other goodies.

Sticks used for roasting food can be wrapped with foil to keep them from catching fire.

Foil wrapped around the outside of pots and pans used for cooking over a campfire will prevent them from getting blackened.

Once the foil has cooled off, make sure you wad it up into a tight little ball and toss it into your garbage bag.

Ants

Ants are very good campers, as can be observed from the fact that they usually construct their ant hill on the one level area suitable for a bed site.

Ants are one good reason for not leaving food in your tent (bears being the other reason). You might have nothing against ants personally and think you wouldn't mind sharing your tent and food with one or two of them. The problem is, they always show up with several hundred relatives. Even that wouldn't be so bad if they were just passing through. But no—you'll find that they persist in holding square dances on your feet, foot races up your legs, cave explorations in your ears, and downhill skiing on your nose. Some of them even take bites out of their host, apparently mistaking him or her for the meat dish of their dinner. The one good thing about ants is that they are a lot smaller than cows.

Axes

I've never found axes to be particularly useful for camping. A large ax is too heavy to carry and a small ax or hatchet is too small to be of much use in gathering firewood. If I can't find enough firewood lying around on the ground, which I usually do, I forget about having a campfire. In the areas where most kid camping occurs, there is usually plenty of loose firewood available. Fingers and toes are often happier, too, if there is no ax on a camping trip. If you decide that you can't survive on a camping trip without an ax, make sure you learn how to use it properly. The Boy Scout *Fieldbook* has an excellent section on the use and care of axes.

ℬ   Backpacking

Backpacking is about the same as kid camping except it's lighter and longer.

Backpackers are fanatics when it comes to weight. Some backpackers will go so far as to clip the little paper tags off their teabags in order to make them lighter. Others will cut most of the handle off their toothbrush for the same reason. I haven't yet seen any backpackers who cut out every other bristle on their toothbrush to make it lighter, but I expect to run into one of them any day now.

Although backpackers may be fanatics about reducing the weight of their packs, the principle they follow is a good one: Take care of the ounces and the pounds will take care of themselves.

And backpackers can't afford to make mistakes. They must have the right gear, the right supplies, the right knowledge and, most important of all, the right attitude. At times they may be thirty miles or more from the nearest road, a hundred miles from the nearest town. Their lives depend upon the contents of their packs, their heads, and their hearts. The experience of kid camping helps to provide those contents.

Backyards

Sleeping out in backyards instructs kid campers in matters of the night.

Once a kid has conquered dark in the backyard, he or she can master it anywhere. There are some rules, however, that should be followed by every kid embarking on his or her first night in the backyard.

First of all, never inform the rest of the family that you are going to sleep out *all* night. When you arrive suddenly back in the house after a couple of hours, your family will want to know the reason.

If you tell them the real reason, that there were two red eyes staring at you from behind a rosebush, everyone will be surprised, never having seen red eyes in the backyard before. The family will troop out to investigate and find that the red eyes are actually only the reflectors on your own bicycle.

This can be embarrassing. To announce your intended adventure, therefore, you should say something like, "I think I'll go out and lie down in my sleeping bag in the backyard for a while." The phrase "a while" covers the whole range of possibilities, from one second to a month. Even so, you should have a good reason worked up for any return to the house before morning. "I felt a few drops of rain" is always a good one.

When you get right down to it, there are only two basic kinds of backyards—yours and somebody else's. If you are sleeping out with a friend in his or her backyard, it is somewhat awkward to retreat into the house if the friend doesn't want to. It can be done, of course. Knock on the back door and tell whoever answers that you've decided to sleep in your friend's bed for the night because your rheumatism is acting up. But by far the best approach is to encourage your friend to make the first move for the inside of his or her house. This can be done in any number of ways. One that almost never fails is to say to your friend, "Say, did you hear what happened to Richy Smith while he was sleeping out in his backyard the other night? He got eaten."

Always remember to tie your dog up before you attempt sleeping out in the backyard for the first time. A warm, wet dog tongue sliding across one's face in the middle of the night can ruin not only one's sleep but one's sleeping bag. More than one sleeping bag has been ripped to shreds by the too-hasty departure of a kid.

The first night I attempted to sleep out by myself in the backyard, something knocked over our garbage can and at the same time let go with the *Aaaaiii!* sound or something like it. I tell you, I was given quite a start. Almost instantly I recognized the culprit of this commotion as our neighbor's cat, but I figured that since I already had quite a start, I might as well go the rest of the way. That's how you figure when you're trying to sleep out in the backyard for the first time.

Beans

Many bad jokes are told about beans on kid camping trips. Since bad jokes are absolutely essential to kid camping trips, as well as to all other kinds of camping trips, beans serve an important function and should never be the item that is forgotten. Cans of so-called pork 'n' beans are best for kid campers. "Hey, I found the pork," a kid will say. "It was hidden under a bean." That is one of the bad jokes.

Bears

There are three basic kinds of bears that the camper needs to know about: national park moocher bears, campground bears, and wild bears.

The park bears who sit along the highway and mooch treats from tourists are, in my opinion, the most dangerous of the three kinds. This is partly because they are so furry and cute. Some tourists can't believe that anything so furry and cute can be dangerous.

Here comes a tourist family driving through the park in their car. Waiting for them is Mr. Moocher Bear. He knows every trick in the book for begging goodies from tourists. He smiles and nods his head in a friendly manner, rests his furry paws on his big pot belly, and lets his long, red tongue loll happily out of the side of his mouth. This act works every time.

"Hey, Pop," yells one of the kids. "Look at the bear!"

"Oh, isn't he cute!" cries the mother. "I always thought bears were ferocious."

"Why, that big, old clown!" says the father. "I'll bet he'd like some marshmallows. I'll feed him some marshmallows right out of my hand and you can take my picture," he tells his wife.

Now this may be a lucky day for the man, in which case he and his family will continue happily on their way, laughing and talking about how the bear ate right out of ol' Pop's hand. Then again, it may be his unlucky day. There will be shouts and yells and screams and ambulance sirens and ranger sirens, and all kinds of commotion. And Moocher Bear will be galloping off through the woods, thinking to himself, "I've got to try to remember—the soft, white things are marshmallows and the long, pink things are fingers. Or is it the other way around?"

What most likely will happen, however, is that the tourist family will be gathered around the bear, tossing him goodies. After he has gulped down the last goody, the bear will look from one member of the family to the other, his eyes asking, "Okay, whose turn is it to toss me a goody?"

"That's all, big fella," the father says. "There isn't any more."

"Wuff!" the bear says, meaning, "All right, I know you're hiding goodies from me. I think I'll just have a look for myself in that sack of yours." And he drops to all fours and starts for the person holding the goody sack.

Shortly, the tourist family is back in their car and roaring off down the highway.

"My goodness!" exclaims the mother. "I don't know why the rangers allow dangerous animals to run around loose like that."

"Ought to be a law against bears!" the man says.

"Let's never go out in the woods again," the children say. "We don't ever want to see a bear again."

Moocher bears, by the way, are found not only in parks. They can turn up along almost any forest highway where tourists are foolish enough to toss them goodies.

Rule: *The cuter and more friendly-seeming the bear, the more dangerous he is. Don't feed him, don't pet him, don't even get out of the car near him. Don't be deceived by his clown act and fetching smile.*

A friend and I were once photographing an orphaned bear cub being raised by a wildlife conservation officer. I was feeding the cub marshmallows so that he would sit for his portrait. While I was waiting for my friend to adjust his camera, I held the marshmallow over my head so that the cub couldn't get it. The cub climbed me as if I were a short tree—a short, *noisy* tree—stood on my shoulders and gobbled down the marshmallow. I still have the scars where his long, cute claws dug into my hide. Even small bears can do a lot of damage to a person!

Campground bears are almost as dangerous as the roadside bears in parks. They like to raid the garbage cans during the night. Once they have finished making their rounds of the garbage cans, they will check out the camp coolers left on picnic tables, popping off aluminum lids as if they were pulltabs on soft drink cans. Bears are *strong*! If you awaken in the night to find a campground bear molesting your camp cooler, don't try to drive him off by yelling and throwing rocks at him. The bear

BEARS

probably won't be afraid of you. Campground bears often will have lost their fear of humans, and that makes them very dangerous.

Rule: *Never keep food in your tent or near where you are sleeping* (unless, of course, you are sleeping in a camper or trailer). In campgrounds, lock your camp cooler and food boxes in the trunk of your car where the bears won't bother them. The bears are after food, not people, and they won't bother you as long as you don't leave food lying around to tempt them.

The truly wild bears are the least dangerous of all. They have retained a healthy fear of people—healthy for you and healthy for the bears. Still, some precaution needs to be taken.

Rule: *Try never to surprise a bear out in the woods, particularly a mother bear with cubs.* Under such circumstances, a mother bear may attack. In order to avoid surprising a bear while you are hiking in the woods, all you have to do is to make some noise every so often—shout to your friends, sing or whistle, whatever strikes your fancy—but make some noise. In wild areas with populations of grizzly bears, hikers often wear bells—called bear bells—to warn of the hikers' approach. The bears will do the rest, which consists of putting as many miles as possible between themselves and the hikers.

Even while camping out in the wilds you should never sleep with your food in your tent or near camp or where bears might be attracted to it. Wild bears are always hungry. They have to work very hard for their food, and they find it impossible to resist camp food left within easy reach. Hang your food bags from a line strung between two trees well away from camp. It should be at least ten feet above the ground so bears can't reach it.

Campers need have no fear of bears out in the woods if the above precautions are taken.

I have associated with bears in the woods for many, many years and we have not yet had even a cross word between us. Not long ago a friend and I were camping deep in the Cascade Mountains of Washington State. We awakened one morning to find fresh tracks where a huge bear had passed by just a few yards from where our sleeping bags had been spread out. He had his own business to tend to and had no interest in poking his nose into our affairs. Finding his tracks so near our camp, however, enriched the morning for us and embedded it forever in our memories.

Bears are an important part of the outdoors, and it would be sad indeed if the only bears were those caged up in zoos.

Bedroll

So you don't have a sleeping bag. No problem. You get to have the fun of making yourself a bedroll. Sleeping bags are fine but they have deprived too many modern kids of the satisfaction of making their own bedrolls. A bedroll is excellent for sleeping in your backyard and for most kid camping trips during the summer.

For your bedroll you'll need two warm blankets. Fold them inside a waterproof groundsheet and attach to your pack.

Beds

When looking for a place to make your bed for the night, try to find a spot that is protected from the wind. Even a slight wind can increase the chill of evenings and mornings.

Next, make sure that your bedsite is not lower than the ground around it, because otherwise, if there is rain during the night, all of the water from the high ground will drain right into your bed. (Lying all night in a pool of cold water tends to make you grouchy in the morning.)

If possible, select a place that will be open to the first rays of

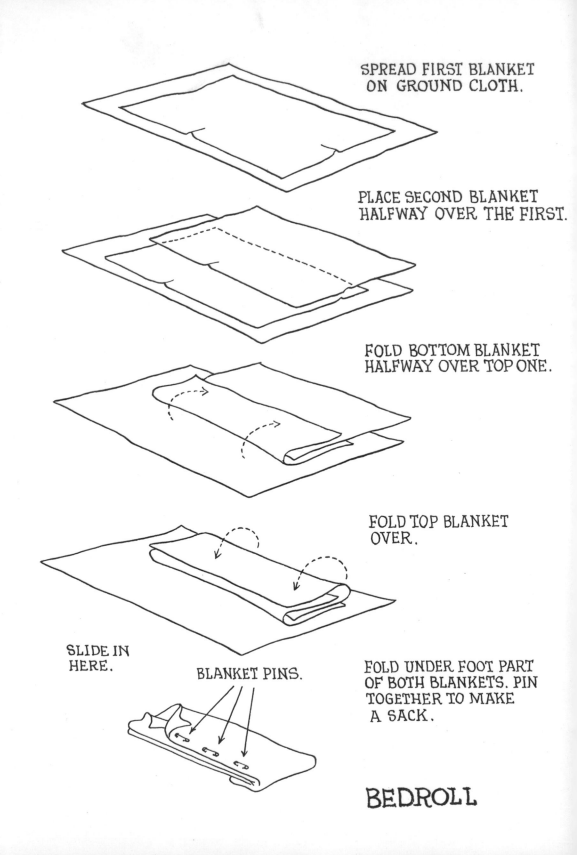

SPREAD FIRST BLANKET ON GROUND CLOTH.

PLACE SECOND BLANKET HALFWAY OVER THE FIRST.

FOLD BOTTOM BLANKET HALFWAY OVER TOP ONE.

FOLD TOP BLANKET OVER.

SLIDE IN HERE.

BLANKET PINS.

FOLD UNDER FOOT PART OF BOTH BLANKETS. PIN TOGETHER TO MAKE A SACK.

BEDROLL

morning sun, since it is always much more pleasant to get up and dressed in a warm, sunny place than one that is shaded and chilly.

Once you have selected just the right spot to spread your groundsheet and roll out your sleeping bag, spend some time removing all the little rocks and sticks from it that may cause you discomfort during the night. A rock the size of a pea will feel like a golf ball by the middle of the night. Before morning it will have grown to the size of a watermelon, and a watermelon is one of the worst things in the world to sleep on. Some campers scoop out some dirt where their hips and shoulders will lie, so the earth will conform to their shape. The problem with this is that it needlessly disturbs the ground cover. It is better simply to place an extra sweater or towel under your sleeping bag in the area where the small of your back will lie. Or use an air mattress.

Now to make your bed. Spread out your groundsheet on the area of ground you have prepared. If you are using a fly sheet for a shelter, make sure the groundsheet doesn't stick out beyond the fly sheet. Otherwise, it will catch the rain coming off the fly sheet and drain it right into your bed. Next comes your insulated pad or air mattress. Your sleeping bag should be shaken out and fluffed up to get plenty of air back into and around the filler. The more still air the insulation captures, the warmer your sleeping bag will be. If the filler isn't fluffed up in the bag so that it can capture air, then it won't keep you warm. Lay your sleeping bag on the insulated pad.

Next, prop your pack up close to the top end of your sleeping bag. This is your bedstand. Place your flashlight in one of the pack pockets within easy reach. You may get thirsty during the night, so set your canteen next to the pack. You also may get chilly during the night, so place a wool shirt or your insulated vest under the pack flap where you can grab it and slip it on if need be. Do the same with your wool cap. If you wear glasses, they can be slipped into a pack pocket out of harm's way.

Your bedroom is ready.

Beef Jerky

Beef jerky is lightweight, nutritious, delicious, convenient—everything but cheap, if you buy it in a store. So you might try making your own. I've tried many different kinds of jerky. Some of it tastes terrible. I had some once that even my dog refused to eat. I don't know whether it was the taste or the look of it he didn't like. But here are a couple of really good recipes for beef jerky. You may wish to experiment a bit with the seasoning to find something that suits your particular taste.

JERKY

Cut lean, raw beef steak or roast into strips ¼ inch thick. Cutting the meat across the grain will make it tender. The meat will be easier to slice if it is slightly frozen (firm but not stiff) in the freezing compartment of your refrigerator. Thread the strips onto a length of clean wire. Meanwhile, a big pot of heavily salted water should be set to boil (¼ cup salt to 1 gallon water). Dip the meat into the boiling brine just barely long enough for the red color to disappear. (This takes only seconds.) Drain meat, then lay it on a platter and salt and pepper it thoroughly. Use pepper generously. Then hang meat to dry in the sun. Put mosquito netting around it to keep flies away.

Drying takes three days in warm weather. Indoors in a warm room, it takes longer. It can also be dried in an oven at very low heat, 140 to 150 degrees. Oven drying takes about eleven hours. Dry the jerky until it is leathery and brittle. Snap off a piece to make sure the middle of the strip is dry.

Kept dry, beef jerky remains good for years.

SEASONED JERKY

Trim as much fat from an inexpensive piece of beef as you can and slice it into strips ¼ inch thick. Marinate the meat for a minimum of a day in:

¼ cup soy sauce
¼ teaspoon pepper
½ teaspoon onion powder
1 teaspoon seasoned salt
¼ teaspoon garlic powder
½ teaspoon liquid smoke
1 tablespoon Worcestershire

Preheat the oven to 175 degrees. Shake excess moisture from the beef strips and lay them out on cake racks or the oven racks, and let them cook slowly for five to six hours. Remove from oven, blot the strips with a paper towel, cool, and store in glass jars or plastic bags.

Jerky is a good trail food, something to snack on while you're hiking, and it can also be used as the meat for stews and other dishes.

Beverages

A hike up a mountain trail on a hot day will make a swig of lukewarm water from your canteen or water bottle taste better than any iced drink in the world, unless of course you happened to find an iced drink along the trail, in which case it tastes considerably better than your lukewarm canteen water. Finding an iced drink along a mountain trail, however, happens so seldom as to be scarcely worth consideration.

Some kid campers of my acquaintance almost always carry a quart of Wyler's lemonade or grape powder. This size makes only enough lemonade for an army so it will last three kid campers about two days, unless the weather is hot and they are thirstier than usual.

Kool-Aid is a favorite of many kid campers. It is light to carry, if the water is not added to it before leaving home.

The best-tasting powdered milk I know of is Milkman. It

comes in foil packets. Each packet makes a quart of milk, which is usually more than is needed at one time, so the opened packet should be placed in a plastic bag that can be closed airtight after each use. Five heaping teaspoons in a Sierra Club cup (see Cup) are about right, but you can mix it to suit your taste by adding more or less powdered milk to your cup of water. You may want to mix your milk a bit richer for use on cold or hot cereal.

In addition to its good taste, Milkman mixes well with cold water.

Rule: *Be sure that all cold water used to mix with drinks is safe to drink.* (See Water.)

Hot chocolate is great for getting a kid camper started on a cold morning. Swiss Miss is a good hot chocolate drink in powder form that mixes with water. Milkman also comes in chocolate flavor.

Since most kid camping trips don't involve hiking any distances, even canned drinks can be packed along. There is pop, of course, but most grocery stores now carry little single-serving size pull-tab cans of different kinds of juices. I hate to say it, but juice is better for kid campers than pop.

Binoculars

What do kids do with binoculars? One of the things kids do with my binoculars is to leave them on rocks and logs alongside trails during rest stops. After we have hiked for about half an hour, I'll say, "Hey, hand me the binoculars. I want to see if that white spot up there on the side of that cliff is a mountain goat." I know that the binoculars have been left somewhere when the kid replies, "Naw, there's no goat up there. Must just be a spot on your glasses."

Besides using binoculars to mark resting places along trails,

BINOCULARS

and bringing considerable delight into the lives of other campers who happen to find them, you can also use binoculars for looking at distant objects. Binoculars are essential for wildlife watching, an activity that enriches any camping trip (see Bird Watching). Binoculars are particularly useful for scanning the terrain up ahead, thereby enabling you to select the easiest route. I've even used binoculars to study the faces of cows in pastures I intended to pass through. If one of the cows has a mean face, I don't go through the pasture.

You can use binoculars to see whether berries up on a side hill are ripe yet. Besides using binoculars to look at large objects in the distance, you can also use them to study small objects nearby—say, an insect within seven or eight feet of you. An ant or grasshopper, enlarged by the binoculars, can provide you with more entertainment than most television shows. (There are no interruptions by commercials, and your average ant or grasshopper is seldom tempted to try out his impersonation of Steve Martin on you.)

Once I even screwed a lens out of my binoculars and used it for starting a fire by focusing the rays of the sun onto some tinder.

Stamped on the case of binoculars, usually just above one of the eyepieces, are some numbers like these: 7 × 35. The 7 indicates that the binoculars will magnify the image of an object seven times. The 35 indicates the diameter of the end lenses in millimeters. The larger the number after the ×, the larger, and heavier, the binoculars, and the more light the lens will let in. As a general rule, the second number should not be more than five times larger than the first. Binoculars stamped with a first number larger than 7 or 8 are not practical for the average camper because the larger the magnification, the more difficult it is to hold the binoculars steady. If the binoculars are not held steady, the image will be blurred. For the camper, 7 × 35 binoculars are just about right.

People sometimes have difficulty finding the object they wish to view once they have put the binoculars to their eyes. The trick is to focus your eyes on the object first, and then, without moving your head or your eyes, lift up the binoculars for viewing. Presto! The object should be right there in the lenses, only seven times larger. You will need to practice with your binoculars in order to "hit" the object with them instantly and every time. Otherwise, you may miss some wonderful close-up glimpses of wildlife while you are sweeping the binoculars up, down and around, trying to find whatever it is you are looking for.

Bird Watching

When I was a youngster, the old woodsman Rancid Crabtree liked to let on to me that he knew the names of all the different species of birds.

"What's that one called?" I would ask, pointing to a large black-and-white bird with a funny tail.

"Hmmmmm," Rancid would say, studying the bird closely. "Wall, now, thet's what you calls your Large Black-and-White Bird with a Funny Tail. Ah'd recognize it anywhar."

I never had any doubt at the time that Rancid knew what he was talking about because the name always matched the bird's appearance exactly. As time went by, however, I began to suspect that the birds might have other names. It turned out that they did.

How do you learn to identify birds? Get yourself a copy of *A Field Guide to the Birds* if you live east of the Mississippi or *A Field Guide to Western Birds* if you live west of the Mississippi. Both books are by Roger Tory Peterson. You should also be able to find a bird book that is devoted exclusively to the birds of your state or region.

Even though bird watchers are quick to deny it, one of the great pleasures of bird watching is simply being able to show off your knowledge of the subject: "By golly," you say to your fellow campers, "there's a Yellow Shafted Flicker."

The most pleasurable aspect of bird study, however, is not mere identification but discovering the personalities of individual birds—the fussbudgets, the thrill seekers, the busybodies, the grouches, the know-it-alls. Birds do have their own distinct personalities.

I would not be at all surprised if most birds were people watchers. "There goes a Yellow-Crested, Freckle-Faced Kid Camper," a know-it-all bird might say.

Blisters

A foot blister is to a hiker what a flat tire is to a bicycle. It makes getting around difficult if not impossible. The hiker must pay close attention to his or her feet if blisters are to be avoided.

First, never start a hike with boots or shoes that are not comfortable and well broken in.

Second, wear a good pair of cotton or wool socks. Halfway through a long hike, change to fresh socks. Two pairs are even better. A light cotton sock close to the skin will absorb perspiration. Wool socks put on over the cotton will provide cushioning. Two pairs of socks also help to reduce friction inside your boots.

Third, as soon as you notice the slightest bit of soreness on one of your feet, sit down and remove your boot and sock and examine the sore spot. If it is red, that means you are about to get a blister.

When you notice a sore spot on one of your feet, cut a patch of moleskin and tape it over the spot with adhesive tape. Put on clean socks.

If you do get a blister—dumb!—wash it with soap and water and pierce it with a needle or pin sterilized in a match flame, slipping the needle in from the edge of the blister so that it can drain. Then cover with a patch of sterile adhesive gauze.

If the blister is allowed to burst—really dumb!—wash it carefully with soap and water and place a patch of sterile gauze over it. You can also cut a hole the size of the blister in a square of moleskin and place that over the blister. A cap cut from moleskin should then be taped over the hole in the first patch. Put on clean, dry socks. The loose skin of the broken blister must be protected so it won't be rubbed and torn. If you notice any rubbing, put a patch of adhesive tape directly over the loose skin of the blister.

If the above procedures for treating blisters don't sound like fun—well, they aren't. The wise camper and hiker takes great care not to get blisters in the first place.

Books, Pamphlets, and Catalogs

Whether you are a boy or a girl camper, the *Fieldbook* of the Boy Scouts of America will provide you with excellent information about a wide variety of outdoor skills. The *Fieldbook* can be purchased for $3.50 at your regional Boy Scout headquarters or at local stores carrying Boy Scout supplies.

The Boy Scouts also publish reprints of camping articles from *Boy's Life* magazine. Several of these reprints include plans for making your own camping equipment: packs, pack frames, tents, stoves, cooking utensils and numerous other good things. These reprints can be purchased at your regional Boy Scout headquarters for about $.50 each.

Worlds to Explore, the handbook for Brownie and Junior Girl Scouts, has an informative and interesting section on outdoor skills for younger girls, or boys for that matter.

Although intended for adult hikers and campers, *The New Complete Walker* by Colin Fletcher is the finest book on backpacking ever written. It's must reading for older kid campers getting ready for serious backpacking.

Besides attempting to sell you their publisher's products, catalogs specializing in outdoor gear and clothing provide interesting and entertaining reading, much useful information and, perhaps most of all, a great deal of wishing on the part of the reader. Here are three of my favorites:

L. L. Bean Catalog, Freeport, ME 04033. Free.

Herter's Catalog, Herter's Inc., Route 2, Mitchell, SD 57301. Price: $1.00 (refunded upon purchase of $10.00 or more).

Recreational Equipment, Inc., R.E.I., 1525 11th Avenue, Seattle, WA 98122. Free.

Boy Scouts

If you have the opportunity to join the Boy Scouts, by all means do so. For most boys, the Scouts provide the greatest range of camping opportunities available, not to mention first-hand and first-rate instruction in all of the outdoor skills. Although girls are not accepted as members of the Boy Scouts, at least not yet, all girls possessed of a love of outdoor life will find the *Fieldbook* and other publications of the Boy Scouts of America to be of enormous value in learning outdoor skills.

C   Cameras

The simpler the camera, the better it is for camping trips. Don't just shoot pictures of the scenery. Take some close-up shots of your camping partners' weatherbeaten faces; get some good close-up pictures of your (ugh) meals (you can use these later to horrify your parents with); and, of course, get some shots of the camp. Remember to have a friend use your camera to shoot some pictures of you. Other camping photographers always promise to give you copies of their pictures but they never do. Here's a good gift idea: give your pals enlarged prints of themselves in camp. Within five years they will consider these pictures priceless, and so will you. If you must forget something, make it the salt or the can opener, but never the camera.

Because they are bulky, cameras that produce instant pictures, such as the Polaroid, never seemed to me to be practical cameras for camping. Recently, though, a kid I was camping with brought along one of these cameras and I was forced to change my mind. Instant picture cameras are, of course, too big for long backpacking trips but for outings of two or three days they are great fun.

Camp Cooks

The feelings of camp cooks are easily hurt. Here are some rules for treating camp cooks properly.

1. While looking at the contents of a pot bubbling over the fire, never say "Ugh" or "Yuck!"

2. If a portion of your food appears to be crawling off your plate, don't call attention to it by screaming.

3. If you are eating in the dark, it is considered both rude and cowardly to shine a flashlight on each bite.

4. Do not butter a rock and pretend you have mistaken it for one of the cook's biscuits.

5. Using pancakes for Frisbees will hurt the cook's feelings and sometimes the other players.

6. When the bacon catches fire, tell the cook, "That's all right, I like my bacon crisp."

7. Never ask, "Are somebody's socks burning?" while the cook is preparing your dinner.

8. It is considered bad manners to suggest singing "Plop Plop Fizz Fizz" around the campfire after supper.

9. Never say, "Gee, I thought we had hash last night," because what you're having tonight probably isn't hash and what you had last night probably wasn't either.

10. Never say, "Boy, you could never get me to eat something like this at home, but out here it tastes pretty good," because the cook will not consider it a compliment.

Campfires

Much nonsense has been written about the difficulty of building a simple little campfire. Just to glance at a set of these preposterous directions you would think from the length and complexity of them that the thing to be built was an atomic submarine rather than a small fire for heat and cooking and staring into and poking at with a stick.

Allow me to describe briefly how I usually build a campfire using only one match. I start by gathering up a handful of tinder and twigs about the size of toothpicks or slightly larger, and placing them in a pile in the middle of my fire site. I then strike a match, which the wind promptly blows out. I strike another match and the wind blows it out. I strike still another match and the wind blows it out.

At this point I mutter several phrases taught to me years ago by a logger who had just dropped an eight-pound metal maul on his big toe. This helps, and the next match ignites the pile of tinder and twigs. As soon as the twigs are burning nicely, I look for some larger sticks, something about the size of pencils, but none is readily available. So, I run around and gather up about

CAMPFIRES

a dozen sticks and rush back to my fire, which by this time has gone out.

I then make another little pile of tinder and twigs and strike a match, which the wind blows out. Three or four matches and a few logger phrases later, I have the pile of twigs burning. The kindling sticks are laid carefully over the burning twigs one at a time. Now, I need some larger pieces of wood, which I immediately set off in search of. By the time I get back, the fire has gone out again and the process must be repeated. Before repeating the process, however, I find that it helps to jump up and down a few times and do a bit of shouting, a practice that does wonders for calming the nerves, and you need calm nerves in order to build a campfire in an efficient manner.

After scarcely more than an hour has passed, I have my fire started, and with only one match, too. Sometimes it might be the fifteenth or twentieth match I try that starts the fire, but it's always one match that does the job. You probably think my method of starting a fire is pretty amazing, but with a little practice you can probably start a campfire almost as well as I. On the other hand, you may prefer the procedure used by the Boy Scouts, Girl Scouts, and Camp Fire Girls for starting a fire. Here's how those smarties do it:

1. Clear all burnable material from around your fireplace until you have a cleared space approximately ten feet in diameter. Select a site that is well away from trees and brush and has no overhanging branches that might be ignited. If the ground has sod on it, cut the sod away and set it aside for use later. (I do this, too.)

2. Gather your tinder, kindling, and firewood and place them near your fire site.

3. Place a pile of tinder in the center of the cleared circle. Then arrange the kindling sticks in the shape of a teepee over the tinder. Next, kneel down so that your body is shielding the fireplace from the wind. Grab a handful of fairly long tinder, strike your match, set the end of the tinder on fire, and use it to start the kindling and other tinder.

4. Feed your fire from the downwind side, adding first more kindling then, gradually, the larger pieces of wood.

In order to help your fire get started, you may want to make fuzz sticks—pieces of kindling sticks that have curls of shavings whittled on them with a knife.

Tinder can be made from dry grasses and weeds or by shredding up the dry inner bark of dead trees.

Firewood should never be taken from live trees. Always use dead trees and branches, and never gather more firewood than you actually need.

When you are ready to break camp, douse your fire thoroughly with water. Then bury all the ashes and pieces of charred wood in the middle of your fire site. If you have removed sod from the area, replace it. As much as possible, replace any ground cover you have removed from the fire site. Scatter any remaining firewood. When you are finished, even an Indian tracker should not be able to tell where your fire was.

That's how the Boy Scouts, Girl Scouts, and Camp Fire Girls do it. Heck, I may even start using their method myself.

Can Opener

The can opener is the item usually forgotten on a camping trip but only if most of the food is in cans. If there are no cans along, each camper will have brought two can openers. No one has ever solved this particular camping mystery, but scientists are working on it. You should also have a can opener on your knife. The U.S. Army-type can opener, which weighs $\frac{1}{8}$ ounce and costs about 25 cents, is one of the last truly great bargains in the world. It really works!

Cans

A canned food is not often carried by backpackers, but it is still an important form of grub in kid camping where the participants must often forage for their food. Since most of their foraging is done in their mothers' kitchens and pantries, much of the available food is likely to be in cans. For some reason, mothers never, never have the good sense to lay in a supply of freeze-dried, foil-packaged camp food. One would think they might be aware that kid camping trips often occur suddenly and without warning.

Canteens

The metal canteen packed on the hip in a canvas holster is not used much by modern campers. They prefer to carry their water in plastic bottles stashed in a convenient pocket on their pack. If you do have a metal canteen though, by all means use it if you want to. Since it hangs from your belt, make sure you are wearing a wide belt so the weight of the canteen won't make the belt dig into your belly. Web belts used by soldiers can be found in military surplus stores, and these belts are perfect for attaching canteen holsters to. You wear it over your regular belt and can unsnap it and take it off without having your pants fall down.

Mixing fruit ade in your water bottle may seem like a good idea at the time, but you'll find that plain old water quenches your thirst better on a long, hot hike.

If you are camping in an area where you aren't sure of the water's safety or whether there is any water at all, you should carry several plastic bottles filled with water from home. (Also see Water.)

Checklist

CLOTHING STUFF

    Boots

    Socks

    Underwear

    Long underwear (for winter camping)

    Pants, shorts

    Belt and/or suspenders

    Heavy wool shirt or sweater

    Light wool shirt

    T-shirt

    Wind parka

    Down- or synthetic-filled vest or jacket

    Gloves or mittens

    Wool watch cap

    Hat or cap with bill

    Rainwear

    Handkerchiefs, bandana

    Sneakers or mocassins

    Swimsuit

COOKING AND EATING STUFF

    Water bottle (canteen)

    Pot with pan top

    Pot lifter

    Frying pan

    Pancake turner

    Cup/bowl

    Tablespoon

    Matches, waterproof

    Foil

    Steel wool scouring pad with soap

    Extra plastic food bags

    Plastic trash bag

Can opener
Dish cloth and towel

SHELTER STUFF

Tent
Flysheet
Groundsheet
Sleeping bag or bedroll
Foam pad or air mattress
Air or foam pillow
Ensolite square for seat

FOOD STUFF

Salt, pepper (in shaker)
Sugar (in container)
Honey (in squeeze tube)
Margarine (in squeeze tube)
Cooking oil
Bisquick
Powdered hot chocolate
Powdered milk
Powdered drink
Trail snacks
Water purification tablets
Breakfast bars
Dehydrated orange juice
Beef jerky
Granola
Foods of your choice

TOILET STUFF

Toothbrush
Toothpaste

All-purpose biodegradable liquid soap
Toilet paper
Mirror
Sun cream
Lip salve
Extra matches
Foot powder
Bar soap
Comb
Small towel

OTHER STUFF

Trowel
Nylon rope
Candle lantern and extra candle
De-fogging spray for glasses
Fishing gear
Compass
Maps
Flashlight with extra batteries and bulb
Sunglasses
Glasses strap
Fishing license
Pocketknife, whetstone
Binoculars or monocular
Camera and film
Needle and thread
Whistle
Insect repellent
Watch
Pedometer

SURVIVAL KIT (See *Emergency Kit*)

Antiseptic ointment
Aspirin
Burn ointment
Gauze
Scissors
Snake-bite kit
Tweezers
Adhesive bandages
Adhesive tape
Moleskin
Salt tablets

Clothes

Any old clothes you have will work fine for kid camping, providing you take enough of them. Since kid camping seldom takes place more than an hour's hike from home, you can always pack on in if you get too wet and cold. A rain jacket of some sort is essential on any kind of camping trip. Campers should always expect rain and cold, and be prepared to dress properly for both.

Sooner or later, kids start going on longer camping trips, either backpacking by themselves or with adults. Backpacking requires much closer attention to clothes than kid camping does. Here are some things you should know:

Socks. Your socks should be either wool or cotton. Many hikers like to wear two pairs of socks to reduce friction inside their boots. They wear a cotton pair next to the skin, because cotton is best for absorbing perspiration. Wool socks are worn over the cotton socks to provide cushioning.

Take extra pairs of socks so that on all-day hikes you can change to dry socks in the middle of the hike. This will help prevent blisters and also make your feet feel good. Don't wear

socks with holes in them or that have been mended on the heels—
the rough mended areas cause blisters.

Dirty socks also cause blisters. On hikes lasting several days,
wash your socks out in the evening and hang them up to dry.
Damp socks can also be fastened to the outside of your pack so
they can dry while you're hiking.

Boots. Running shoes and tennis shoes or sneakers are fine
for most overnight hikes. On backpacking trips where you hike
all day for several days over steep, rocky trails, you should
wear leather boots or shoes that are high enough to support
and protect your ankles. The soles should be sturdy but flexible.
The fewer the seams on the boot, the more watertight it will be.
Boots can be waterproofed by treating them with oil, grease, or a
mixture of wax and silicon. Most boots come with a tag indicating
what waterproofer should be used on them.

It is extremely important that a hiker's boots fit properly. When
you start down a steep trail or mountainside, your feet will slide
forward in your boots. There should be enough room so that
your toes don't press against the front of the boot. When you
are buying a new pair of boots, stand toes-down on the slanted
side of two of those little stools shoe clerks use for trying shoes
on customers. If your toes touch the front of the boot, you need
a larger pair. While checking the fit, always wear the socks, one
or two pair, that you plan on using with the boot. With your
socks on, you should be able to slip a finger between your heel
and the back of the boot.

Be sure your boots are well broken in before wearing them on
a long hike.

Never dry your boots close to a campfire. I remember the
time a kid named Kenny was drying his boots in this manner
and suddenly somebody shouted, "Kenny, your boots are smok-
ing!" Thinking to save Kenny's boots, another kid grabbed them
and stuck them in the cold creek to cool off. The toes popped
right out of Kenny's boots. None of us ever again dried our
boots by the fire.

Underwear. Cotton underwear is best for hiking, because it absorbs perspiration best. Carry an extra set or two of underwear, and change every day. Wash out and dry your underwear when you do your socks.

Long underwear is seldom needed, except possibly for winter camping.

Pants. Jeans are fine for most camping trips. You may also want to take along a pair of cutoffs or hiking shorts. Wool pants are good for cold, wet weather. A pair of wool pants from one of your father's or uncle's old wool suits can be chopped off to fit you.

Shirts and Sweaters. Experienced campers and hikers prefer to dress in layers. The first layer will be a cotton T-shirt; the next layer, a light wool shirt; the next, a heavy wool shirt or sweater; the next, an insulated vest; and the last layer, a parka shell. If the camper feels too cool, a layer is added; if too warm, a layer is removed.

Insulated Vests. These are lightweight and super warm. They are insulated either with down from waterfowl or with artificial fillers of various kinds. A down-filled vest can be wadded up into a ball not much larger than a grapefruit and stuffed into your pack. Down-filled vests, sweaters, and jackets are expensive, however, and difficult to dry once they become wet. Vests filled with artificial insulators are bulkier but less expensive, and they dry faster. Both will keep you warm.

Parka. This is an essential item on any overnight trip or even a day hike. A parka is a loose-fitting jacket with a hood. It should be rainproof and windproof, and have both a zipper and snaps. (If the zipper becomes stuck, or broken, as zippers tend to do, you can still keep the parka closed with the snaps.) Some parkas are lined. Unlined parkas are called parka shells. The parka shell is usually sufficient, since you can wear all your layers including the insulated vest under it if the weather gets really cold.

Gloves. Wool gloves add very little to the weight of a pack and are very nice to have in cold weather. They make good potholders too.

Poncho. A poncho is kind of a tent you can walk in. It is a large sheet of waterproof fabric with a hole in the middle of it for your head. A hood with a drawstring is attached. There are no sleeves. The poncho will hang down over your knees in front and cover your pack behind. The poncho can also be turned into an emergency shelter or used for a groundsheet under your sleeping bag. For that matter, groundsheets can be used for ponchos. For most trips, however, a good parka shell is generally lighter and more comfortable than a poncho.

Bandana. Get yourself a large bandana. It will have dozens of different uses—as a washrag, potholder, berry bucket, sweatband, and hat. You can even wear it around your neck.

Hat or Cap. Either will protect the top of your head from the sun and help keep your body heat in when weather turns cold. The brim or bill will keep the sun out of your eyes. If you wear glasses, as I do, a broad brim or long bill is absolutely essential to keep your spectacles from getting wet in the rain.

A wool watch cap, such as sailors wear, or a plain old wool stocking cap is an essential item in your camp wardrobe. A wool cap will help prevent your body heat from escaping through the top of your head on cool days. No kidding.

Companions

Never go hiking alone. Even the most careful hiker will occasionally have an accident. A sprained ankle, enough of a nuisance when it befalls you at home, can be deadly serious when it occurs out on the trail. You may trip and bump your head on a rock. Or you may get lost. If you knew what accidents were going to happen, they wouldn't be accidents. (Ever hear anybody say, "I think I'll stroll over into the woods there and see if I can't get lost"?) Companions can help you out of your predicament either by giving direct assistance or going for help.

One time my friend Vern and I were out in the woods near our homes picking berries. Both of us knew the woods as well as we knew our own bedrooms (although the woods were less messy). There was no chance of our getting lost, since we both knew all the various landmarks. All we had to do was look around and pick out a landmark and we would instantly know where we were and the way home. But suddenly, as I was wandering along intent on the next patch of ripe dewberries, *zap!* A hornet, traveling at terrific speed, hit me right between the eyes with such force I was almost knocked flat on my back. By the time I realized what had happened, I was already dizzy and sick, and my eyes were beginning to swell shut. My head felt as if someone were dribbling it around a basketball court and doing trick shots with it. Then something happened I thought was impossible: I started feeling a whole lot worse. I might have made it out of the woods without Vern's help, but probably not. Vern certainly didn't think so, because forever after he referred to the incident as "The time I saved your life." Usually, he referred to it in this manner when we were sharing a box of Cracker Jack and arguing over who would get the prize.

Companions, of course, are nice to have along on hikes and camping trips for reasons other than safety. There's someone around to laugh at your jokes, for instance. Companions also share the misery that is so much a part of real camping: cold, rain, insects, dark, etc. And having a share of the misery is certainly much better than having all of it.

There are all kinds of companions: good companions, bad companions, serious companions, funny companions, old companions, young companions, girl companions, boy companions, and all different sizes and colors of companions. I have on occasion found myself on a camping trip with a bad companion. But even a bad companion is 1,574 times better than no companion at all, and you can never tell when an emergency might turn a bad companion into a good companion.

Compass

A compass is useful in preventing you from becoming lost, provided that it is used properly. On the other hand, it does little good for a compass to indicate which direction is north if you haven't the foggiest notion whether you are supposed to be going north or south, east or west. Therefore, it is important for you to learn how to use both maps and compass. The Boy Scout *Fieldbook* is a good place to start learning about maps and compasses. Both the Boy Scouts and Girl Scouts have games they play with compasses to provide practice in using them correctly. Even if you aren't a Scout, you and your friends can work up your own compass games. One person hides an object and then writes out a set of compass directions for finding the object. The other players, using their compasses, follow these directions, the winner being the person who finds the object first. Needless to say, it is essential that the person who hides the object know how to read a compass.

Cooking

A typical backpacker's meal will go something like this: A half-hour or so before reaching camp, the backpacker will dump a package of freeze-dried stew into a plastic bag, slosh in a bit of water from the water bottle, tie the bag shut and place it in a side pocket of the pack. As soon as he or she arrives at the camping place for the night, the camp stove is started and a pot of water put on to heat. By the time the camp is set up, the water is boiling. The freeze-dried stew, which will have absorbed the water in the bag, is dumped onto a plate and mixed with boiling water. Some more boiling water is dumped over a tea bag, instant coffee, or instant chocolate in the Sierra Club cup (see Cups). The backpacker eats the stew, drinks the beverage, has a bit of dried fruit for dessert, washes dishes and turns in. All very fast, neat, and efficient.

Well *blah*, I say. Maybe I would handle my camp cooking like that if I were being pursued through the woods by a mob of armed criminals. Or on a week-long outing with 100 miles to cover. But not otherwise. For me, much of the fun in camping comes from the cooking. This is particularly true for kid camping, where there is always plenty of time and no need to rush. (If there's little time and a need to rush, then what's being done isn't kid camping but some other kind.)

Since kid camping by its very nature won't involve a hike of more than a mile or two from home, and may even take place in the backyard, freeze-dried foods manufactured for backpackers are unnecessary, although you might want to try a package or two each trip for experimental purposes. That way, by the time you are ready for long-distance backpacking you will know which freeze-dried foods you like best and how to prepare them. For kid camping, though, you will carry the basic foods foraged out of the refrigerator or pantry at home. Here is a typical list of foods for a kid camping trip:

> Potatoes, 4 raw
> Marshmallows, 1 package
> Fruit ade, 4 packages
> Potato chips, 2 packages
> Pop, in cans, 4
> Onions, 2
> Candy bars, 6
> Marshmallows, 1 package
> Eggs, 1 dozen
> Bacon, 1 pound
> Wieners, 1 pound
> Hot dog buns, 1 package
> Fruit cocktail, 2 cans
> Bisquick, 1 box
> Marshmallows, 1 package

Sugar, 2 cups
Bread, 1 loaf, sliced
Margarine, ¼ pound
Peanut butter, 1 jar
Jelly, 1 jar
Maple syrup, 1 jar (for the pancakes)
Marshmallows, 1 package
Apples, 4
Oranges, 4
Carrots, 0
Bananas, 4 (mushed)
Salt
Pepper
Beef jerky
Pork 'n' beans, 1 can
Gorp

Have I forgotten anything? Oh yes, be sure and take plenty of marshmallows. For a two-night trip, just double the quantities on the list. I know this doesn't sound like much grub for one night, but keep in mind that each of the other campers will be bringing a similar amount. Even if you do run out, you won't be so far from home that you'll starve, particularly if you're camped in the backyard.

There are several hundred camp food recipes I could give you, but inventing your own is half the fun. However, there are some that every kid camper must try. Here they are:

Potatoes baked in the coals. This is not a very catchy name but it is descriptive. Wash whole, unpeeled potatoes and drop them into the coals of the cooking fire. Make sure they are completely covered with coals; otherwise, they burn. You don't really even have to wash the potatoes. Coal-baked spuds are delicious with just a bit of salt, fantastic with a glob of margarine.

Bread Twist. Pour a bit of water into your plastic bag of Bisquick and mix up a nice thick dough using a clean stick to stir with. Haul out your wad of dough and work it out into a rope-like shape about a foot long. Wrap this around a clean stick a couple of inches in diameter. Jam the stick in the ground or brace it up so it slants out over the coals at about a 45-degree angle, which is halfway between straight up and flat. Don't get the twist too close to the coals or it will burn. Turn the stick occasionally so the twist bakes on all sides. When the bread has baked golden brown, peel it from the stick and eat it with margarine and jelly.

Flapjacks. Mix up your batter in a plastic bag following the directions on the Bisquick box. Now pour the batter into a lightly greased skillet until the bottom is covered. When the top of the flapjack is covered with bubbles, that means it is ready to turn. At this point, you grab the handle of the frying pan, stand up, and announce, "Okay, gang, watch this." Then with a quick underhand tossing motion ending in an abrupt stop, you flip the flapjack over in the air. Neat, huh?

Note: A hair in your flapjack should not be great cause for concern; a soggy flapjack in your hair, on the other hand, is a terrible mess. Beginning camp cooks should always clean poorly flipped pancakes off their shoes, shoulders, heads, tents and friends. These flapjacks should be discarded; don't try to feed them to your friends for lunch, even though they laughed at you.

Grilled Steak Cubes. Cut the steak into chunks, slip the chunks on a stick and broil over the coals in the same manner as bread twist, turning the stick every so often. Alternate the chunks with onion and pieces of green pepper and you'll have shish kebab. Grilled steak cubes may be eaten directly from stick, after they have cooled enough not to burn you.

Roast Chicken. For this you need a length of wire 5 or 6 feet long, aluminum foil, and one whole frying or roasting chicken. Salt the chicken on the inside. Secure the chicken to one end of the wire in the manner of wrapping up a package. Lean a slender pole up over the crosspiece of your cooking spit (see Cooking Spit) so that the high end is directly over your bed of coals (see Cooking Fire). Attach the wire to the pole so that the chicken is suspended about a foot over the coals. Now take a

COOKING

sheet of foil and form a hood over the top and around the sides of the chicken. The foil should be about six inches from the chicken. Direct heat from the fire will roast the bottom part of the chicken, and reflected heat from the hood will roast the top and sides. Finally, make a foil pan and place it on the coals directly under the chicken to catch the drippings, which can then be used to baste the bird.

If you can't forage a chicken, use this same method to bake a Spam.

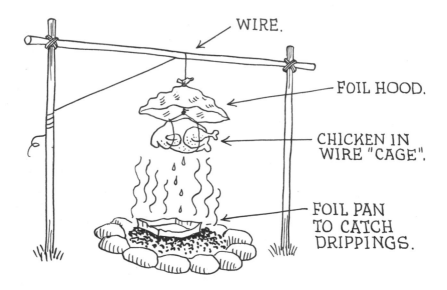

WIRE.

FOIL HOOD.

CHICKEN IN WIRE "CAGE".

FOIL PAN TO CATCH DRIPPINGS.

Cooking Fire

Camping books often recommend that a fire be allowed to burn down into a nice bed of coals to be used for cooking. The problem I encountered with this method is that the coals often burn out before the food is cooked. Then you have to start up the fire again to get more coals. While this is being done you have to set your dinner aside and someone will accidentally step right in the middle of it and then you have to take time to scrape off his or her shoe and try to get most of the supper back into the pan, and it's a big nuisance. Or your dog will come along and sample the supper and that cuts down on everybody else's share, and there are even a few picky campers who refuse to eat dinner after a dog has sampled it unless, of course, the dish you're serving is particularly good.

To avoid these complications, what you do is to build a cooking area, usually just a half circle of flat rocks next to your regular campfire. You use a stick to rake coals from the fire into your cooking area. As long as you feed wood to it, the fire will keep on producing coals and you'll have a steady supply for your cooking. This arrangement is called a "keyhole fire." It doesn't really look like a keyhole; it just looks like a fire with the coals raked out to the side of it. But use this method for maintaining a steady supply of cooking coals.

You may want to practice your camp cooking out in the backyard. You may even be doing your camping in the backyard, so you'll naturally have to do your camp cooking there. Chances are your folks wouldn't be too happy about your building a campfire in the middle of the lawn, so you'll have to use charcoal. If you don't have a charcoal brazier handy, you can put some sand (clean cat litter can be used) in the bottom of an old metal tub or pan or some other metal container and use that.

Here's a way to start the charcoal without using starting fluids, which can be dangerous. Cut the top and bottom out of a one-gallon tin can. Punch holes all around the bottom edge of the can. Set the can in the brazier. Wad up a sheet of newspaper and put it in the bottom of the can. Place the cubes of charcoal on top of the paper. Lift up the can on one side and light the paper. If more draft is needed, prop up one edge of the can with a cube of charcoal. In about 30 minutes the charcoal will be hot. Remove the can with a pair of tongs, pliers, or a couple of sticks. Spread the glowing charcoal around a bit and you're ready to start cooking.

WARNING! Never use charcoal in the house—in the fireplace, for example—or in any other closed area, because the burning charcoal gives off a deadly gas called carbon monoxide. You can't see or smell the gas and that makes it even more dangerous.

Cooking Spit

A spit for cooking over a campfire is worthwhile building any time you plan on spending several days at one camp.

Traditionally, forked sticks have been used for uprights, but any sturdy straight sticks will work if you notch them at the place where they touch the crosspiece. Wire or heavy twine can be used to fasten the crosspiece to the uprights, but if twine is used the uprights should be far enough from the flames that it won't burn. The uprights should be about 3 feet high. S-hooks (see S-Hooks) are used to hang pots from the crosspiece, one end of which should extend a couple feet beyond the fire to provide a place to hang pots away from the heat. The crosspiece can be wrapped in foil to keep it from burning.

Cooking Utensils

The simplest way to acquire most of the utensils you need for camp cooking is to go out and buy a camp cook kit. Aluminum camp cook kits are lightweight and compact. The smaller pots and pans nest inside the largest pot, with the frying pan serving as the lid for the kit.

I have two aluminum cook kits. One is used for group camping and has a capacity to serve up to ten people. The other one is a backpacking cook kit and can handle the cooking for two people. It has its own little gas stove, two pots, and a frying

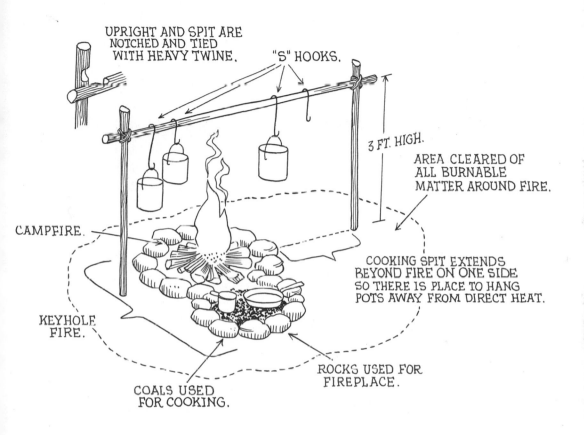

UPRIGHT AND SPIT ARE
NOTCHED AND TIED
WITH HEAVY TWINE.

"S" HOOKS.

3 FT. HIGH.

AREA CLEARED OF
ALL BURNABLE
MATTER AROUND FIRE.

CAMPFIRE.

COOKING SPIT EXTENDS
BEYOND FIRE ON ONE SIDE
SO THERE IS PLACE TO HANG
POTS AWAY FROM DIRECT HEAT.

KEYHOLE
FIRE.

ROCKS USED FOR
FIREPLACE.

COALS USED
FOR COOKING.

COOKING SPIT

pan. Since kid camping has a way of turning into backpacking, you will eventually want to acquire one of the smaller cook kits. With stove, they cost about $40 at present prices.

If you don't have an extra $40 lying about at the moment, you can scrounge up a perfectly adequate cook kit for kid camping. Chances are your mother has several old pots and pans she will be willing to donate to a good cause. These pots and pans will no doubt have plastic handles on them. The plastic will melt over a campfire, and therefore must be removed, either with a few deft turns of a screwdriver or a few deft whacks with a hammer. If the pots don't have bails (arched handles) already on them, make some from wire coat hangers. The bails are needed for hanging the pots over the fire and as handles. Rather than trying to replace the straight plastic handles on your pots, you should buy a pot lifter, available in most outdoor sporting goods departments. The pot lifter, which works something like pliers, grips the top edge of the pot and does away with the need for handles.

If you can't find any old pots around the house, you can attach wire bails to 1-pound, 2-pound, and 3-pound coffee cans or similar-size cans that have contained food. Avoid using as pots any cans that may have contained something other than food.

Aluminum foil is a cook kit all by itself (see Aluminum Foil).

Camp chefs should always include a set of S-hooks in their cook kits. The S-hooks are used to hang pots from the cooking spit. Otherwise, the cook has to lift up one end of the cooking spit in order to slide the bail of a pot on or off. A set of four hooks ranging in length from 4 inches to 10 inches should be sufficient. The short hooks hold the pot higher above the fire and the longer hooks, lower. The S-hooks should be made out of wire heavy enough that the weight of a pot of water won't straighten out the S. (See S-Hooks.)

Other utensils needed for your cook kit are:

1 Pancake turner. Handy for frying fish, hash-brown potatoes, french toast, etc. Can also be used for turning pancakes.

1 Can opener, miniature, U.S. Army type.

1 Tablespoon

1 Salt and pepper shaker. Buy one designed for use by campers. Salt goes in one end, pepper in the other. Cap on end turns to close and open holes.

1 Sugar container. A small plastic box with vacuum-seal lid such as sold by Tupperware works best. Put heavy rubber bands around box to make sure it doesn't pop open in pack.

1 Margarine container. Use plastic squirt tube manufactured especially for backpackers. A clip allows the bottom of the tube to be opened for filling and then resealed. Camper unscrews cap on top of tube to squirt out margarine. Each tube holds ¼ pound margarine.

1 Honey or jam container. Use squirt tube.

1 Potholder

1 Waterproof matchsafe (See Matches.)

Cows

What have cows to do with camping? Everything. Strangely enough, most books on camping will warn about such problems as bears, rattlesnakes and the like, but none ever mentions cows. To my mind, cows are one of the great nuisances of the world. They are everywhere. I have not the slightest doubt that the first expedition of mountain climbers to scale Mount Everest found a cow at the summit happily chewing her cud. Probably the reason the mountain climbers never reported the cow is that they were too ashamed to.

Just by her very presence a cow can destroy even the most noble and heroic act. Many is the time that I have hiked into the trackless wilderness, certain that no one had ever trod that same ground before. Then as I shucked off my pack and sat down to drink in the glory of the wilderness, a cow would walk by, look at me and say, "Moooooo." Somehow the wilderness isn't the same after that.

Cows are of special concern to kid campers. Since kids generally don't as a rule have a car of their own to drive off to distant places, they must find campsites close to home. Among the most available camping places close to home are pastures. And pastures, it so happens, are the natural habitat of cows. Any time they are not climbing Mount Everest or tracking up the wilderness, cows are vacationing in pastures and planning their next outing.

I wish I could tell you of a good cow repellent to buy, but as far as I know there isn't any. You just have to put up with cows.

The sensible kid camper will arrange to have a fence between him and the cows at all times. The farmer who gives you permission to camp on his property will usually direct you to an area that his cows at the moment are fenced out of. Keep in mind that the cows have probably been in the area at one time or another. Therefore you should watch where you step and where you toss down your sleeping bag. To cows, the whole world is a bathroom.

Farmers don't understand cows. Otherwise, why would they keep them around? One time when we were kids my friend Retch and I were fishing a creek that ran through a pasture, and a cow suddenly charged out of the brush and took after us. She chased us across the creek, where there were still more cows, and they all jumped up and joined in with the first cow. Pretty soon there were cows racing in every direction and we became confused about which cows were chasing us and which were just coming along for the fun of it. We would run in one direction and a cow would cut us off, and then we would run in another direction and there would be a squad of cows stationed there, and it was all very wild and frantic. Finally the farmer came out of his barn and saw the cows chasing us. "Hey!" he yelled, "you boys stop bothering those cows!" As I say, farmers just don't understand cows.

Crawly Things

You never see crawly things, you just feel them. Ants, for example, aren't crawly things. Ants are ants. You can see them. Even spiders and snakes are not crawly things, because you can see them.

The only way you know a crawly thing is around is if you feel it or somebody else yells, "*Aaaaiii!* I just felt a crawly thing on me!"

I'm the only person I know of who was ever placed in danger by a crawly thing. At the time I was ten years old and sleeping out in a tent with my cousin, Buck, who was fourteen. I had often heard that Buck was not only totally fearless but also knew everything there was to know about camping out. Since Buck was the person I often heard this from, I had no reason to doubt it. My surprise was considerable, therefore, when, in the middle of the night, Buck gave a startled yelp, leaped up, and began beating his sleeping bag with one of his boots.

"What's wrong, Buck?" I shouted. "What's wrong?"

"A crawly thing nearly got me!" he said, panting. "But I think I squashed it. Shine that flashlight over here."

In the beam of the flashlight, Buck slowly lifted his boot, and both of us peered under it. There, squashed flat, greenish, still partly coiled, lay the frayed end of a sleeping bag drawstring.

That was when I was placed in danger. Have you ever laughed so hard you couldn't stop, even though somebody bigger than you was making threats on your life? If not, you've never seen anybody try to squash the frayed end of a sleeping bag drawstring with a boot.

I suspect most crawly things are nothing more than the frayed ends of sleeping bag drawstrings and the like. The problem is that whenever I feel a crawly thing on me I seem unable to suspect anything but snakes and spiders.

Crouch Hop

The crouch hop comes in handy when you are pounding in a tent stake with a flat rock and some of your fingers get between the stake and the rock. I have never heard a doctor say in just what way the crouch hop soothes the injured fingers, but since almost everybody uses it, some relief must be obtained. The way you perform the crouch hop is this: First, you jerk up the injured fingers and look at them briefly, although often this first step is eliminated in favor of getting directly into the crouch hop. Next, you place your injured hand between your knees and hunch over. Then you begin hopping around in ever-expanding circles until the pain lets up. While doing the crouch hop, some persons like to chant "Ooooo! Ow! Ow! Ouch! Ooooo! Ow! Ow! Ouch!" Adults often use other chants but this one is best for kids.

Cups

Buy yourself the famous stainless steel Sierra Club cup. This cup is the badge of the serious camper, and there are no campers more serious than kid campers. The cup should be carried on your belt or attached to an easily reached place on the outside of your pack. If you are in an area where the streams are pure enough to drink from, the cup will save you from having to flop down on your belly in order to drink. The cup is often used as a plate by backpackers; they'll have a course of stew in the cup and then a course of beverage and then another course of stew. Personally, I've never cared for this practice since the course of beverage often tastes like the course of stew. Also, I don't like to find chunks of carrot floating in my hot chocolate. I don't like to find chunks of carrots floating in anything, but especially not my hot chocolate.

CROUCH HOP

Dark—And What to Do About It

Sooner or later on every kid camping trip the unexpected happens—it gets dark. Night always came as a great surprise to me when I was a kid camper. Everything would be going along fine and then, suddenly, the sun would go down.

"Hey, it's starting to get dark," one of my friends would say.

"Yeah," I would reply calmly, even as deep inside me a little voice was crying out "No! It can't be! *Aaaaiii!*" The little voice belonged to my liver. I had a chicken liver.

Dark never bothered me too much when it was outside the windows of my house or even when it was filling up my bedroom at night. But on camping trips, the whole world seemed to be buried under darkness. On my early camping trips I was always afraid that I wouldn't wake up in the morning, and several times I didn't. After all, you can't wake up if you haven't gone to sleep.

The nights were long on those camping trips. Seconds ticked by like centuries; minutes came and went like ice ages. Then, after scarcely a billion years had passed, the first light of dawn would slide up the eastern sky and a short while later the sunlight would come walking down the trees to our camp. "Hooray!" my chicken liver would shout. "We made it through the night. Gee, that wasn't so bad, was it?"

It's very easy to let fear of the dark ruin camping out for you. So, don't fight it. Get yourself a camping night light. Since there are no electrical outlets in any place worthy of the name "campsite," what you need is a little candle lantern. You can make one yourself out of a tin can or buy one. Even though I am not in the least bothered by the dark on camping trips anymore—well, maybe just a bit—I purchased a neat little fold-up candle lantern a while back and it works like a charm as a night light. Special long-burning candles can be purchased for the lantern. They give off a surprising amount of light. As the saying goes, it is better to light one candle than to curse the darkness. And by the way, if you're afraid you might be teased for using a candle lantern, let me point out that I camp with some pretty rough and rugged individuals and not once have I heard them crack a single joke about my candle lantern. As they are quick to explain, they are not bothered at all by the dark, heh, heh, but it's nice to have a bit of light around just in case they need to find something during the night.

One word of caution: Since candle lanterns give off light by means of flame, you must be extremely careful to hang up the lantern in such a way that it can't fall and so there is nothing close to it that might catch fire.

Your flashlight should be kept within easy reach during the night (see Flashlights). It is not necessary, as some kid campers believe, to keep it clutched in a hand.

There is a great variety of lanterns on the market nowadays, including propane, white gas, and battery models. Although these lanterns may have their uses in the outdoors, they don't add much to kid camping and are best avoided. Gas lanterns can be dangerous. A good flashlight and a candle lantern are what you need for the dark.

The dark can be dangerous, but only if you lose your head and go tearing off through the middle of it. I did this a few times as a kid and was lucky enough to pull through with only minor changes in my anatomy. When I was sixteen a friend and I were bivouacked for the night on a ridge high up in the Rocky Mountains. A storm came up and lightning struck right next to our camp. Both of us thought the next bolt was going to hit us dead center, so we instantly lost our heads and peeled off down the side of the mountain in pitch darkness. I stopped in time but my friend ran right off over a cliff. He landed so hard, he said later, he thought he would have to go through the rest of his life with his legs sticking out of his armpits. Both of us learned right then that there may be good reason for moving around through the woods in the dark, but to walk slowly and carry a good flashlight.

Directions—Or, How to Get Yourself Lost in the Woods

Getting lost in the woods is usually a lot of fun. The fun ceases as soon as you are lost, however, and is replaced by fear. Fear sometimes makes the lost person think with his or her feet, and feet, let's face it, are not all that smart. The only idea feet can ever come up with for getting their person unlost is to start moving wildly about in half a dozen different directions. What the lost person must think with is his or her head. And here is what must be thought about:

When you first discover that you are lost, you are probably not badly lost. At worst, you are probably no more than a mile from the nearest road. So try not to get any more lost than you are. That is the first rule. Select a large landmark such as a tree or rock that you can see for a considerable distance. Then, as you go out to look for a road or trail or fence that can lead you back to civilization, never go beyond sight of your landmark and, if you are unsuccessful in your scouting efforts, return to it. That way even if you can't find your way out, you won't become *more* lost and it will be easier for someone to find you. A shout every five minutes or so will help guide the searchers to you.

If you are very lost, helicopters and planes will be sent out to look for you. The best thing to use for attracting their attention is a mirror, which you should carry in your emergency kit (see Emergency Kit). If you don't have the kit along, use any shiny object, such as the bottom of a berry pail, to flash at the airplanes. If you don't have a shiny object, tie your handkerchief, T-shirt or any brightly colored cloth to a stick and wave it.

You can even build a small fire and throw handfuls of damp leaves on it to create smoke, a tiny plume of which can be seen from great distances. Use the standard safety procedures for fire building, since being lost is bad enough; you don't want to be lost in a forest fire.

If you do have to stay out overnight, find a place close to your landmark where you are protected from the wind, because the wind can make you much colder than you already are. Try to stay dry if it rains. Get under a tree with thick foliage (see Lightning) or build a simple lean-to.

Unless you panic upon discovering that you are lost, searchers shouldn't have much trouble finding you.

The greatest danger to the life of a lost camper is not wild animals or starving but loss of body heat. This is called hypothermia. (See Hypothermia.) Body heat can be lost by rushing frantically about and using up energy. It is important to be calm and to slow down so that your energy can be used for heat.

Here are some easy ways to get lost in the woods:

1. Wandering aimlessly without paying attention to where you are going or to where you have been. A person who *doesn't* want to become lost will take the trouble to pick out landmarks along the way so he or she can use them to find the way back out. The landmarks should be looked at back over your shoulder, because they sometimes appear quite different from the going side than from the returning side. And the returning side of a landmark is what the hiker should be most interested in.

2. Taking shortcuts. The camper or hiker thinks some time can be saved by getting off the trail and cutting through the woods to his or her intended destination. This is an almost certain way to get lost. Considerable time and study have gone into laying out the routes of trails and if the best way to get to the place where the trail leads were off through the woods, then the trail would go off through the woods. Don't try to outguess the trailmakers—unless, of course, you want to get lost.

3. Following game trails. Keep in mind that what may be home to a deer may be lost to you. I have spent much of my life following game trails, and though the animals that made the trails probably had some good reason for them, I've seldom been able to discover the reason. Sometimes the game trails will just stop way off in the woods someplace, and when I start back I discover that what seemed like one game trail is actually a dozen trails, branching off in all directions. Since wild animals don't often seek out the company of people, it is unlikely that

game trails will lead you to people. If you are already lost, don't follow game trails.

4. The most common method for getting lost is to walk "just a little ways" off a road or trail to pick some berries or to look at something. Because the camper or hiker is going into the woods "just a little ways," he or she doesn't think it necessary to pay attention to the landmarks needed to find the way back out. Keep in mind that in the woods you have to pay attention all the time, even if you're going "just a little ways." No hiker or camper should take more than five steps into the woods without an extra sweater or wool shirt, a pocket knife, and waterproof matches. (See Emergency Kit.)

Dogs

At least one dog must go along on every kid camping trip. If you don't have a dog, try to borrow one. Kid camping just isn't kid camping without a dog.

Never take more than three dogs, though, because then you have a dog camping trip, and that's practically no fun at all.

Even one dog, if he puts his mind to it, can cause enough trouble for all the campers to get their full share and a little extra. He'll jump in the creek, roll in the mud, and then seek out the nearest sleeping bag to shake himself off on. He'll chew up one person's sock and run off with another one's boot. He'll sit down in somebody else's supper. ("Oh, pardon me," he'll say, glancing around. "I do hope you were finished with that plate of pork 'n' beans.")

Of course, it's hard work for just one dog to supply an excess of trouble for a whole camp. It's much better if you take two dogs along and let them divide the work between them.

My dog, Strange, never missed one of my kid camping trips. Sometimes I'd try to sneak off without him, but he always caught me. "Yay hoo!" he would shout. "Another camping trip! Hold up a sec while I pack a bone, and I'll be ready to go."

Strange spoke only in dog talk, of course. I understood dog talk but pretended to Strange that I didn't. Otherwise he would never have shut up.

Strange was a chow hound. He was always hungry. He could have eaten a whole cow for dinner and said afterwards that he was glad he had saved room for dessert. His big worry on our camping trips was that he would starve to death. "Did you bring plenty of food for me?" he would ask. "No, you probably didn't! You're always forgetting to bring enough food! I'm going to starve out here in the wilds, I just know it!"

Whenever a wiener I was roasting over the campfire accidentally fell in the dirt, Strange would rush in and grab it. Then he would put on a big show, pretending that the wiener had been escaping and he had captured it for me. All the time, of course, he would be going slobber, slobber, slobber on the wiener as fast as he could.

Strange also liked to masquerade as my loyal protector, but his little act never fooled me. As soon as I was settled in my sleeping bag, he would walk over, look down into my eyes, and say, "You get some sleep, Boss. I'll stand guard."

There was no way a person could get much sleep with Strange standing guard. About the time I was ready to drift off, he would stare wildly out into the dark and announce, "Oh, oh, there's *something* out there." My eyes would pop open, my ears flare out. "Oh, my gosh!" Strange would whine. "It's got hair a foot long all over it, hideous claws and fangs and red eyes and—" At that he would dive into my sleeping bag and curl up into a shivering, whining ball at my feet. By then, of course, there would be quite a bit of shivering if not whining going on in the rest of my sleeping bag and in all the other campers' sleeping bags as well.

"What is it?" one of my friends would hiss.

"I don't know for sure but it's got hair a foot long all over it and hideous fangs and claws and red eyes."

"Ohhhh no!" my friend would moan. "I just knew something like this was going to happen!"

Sounds of the monster's approach would reach our ears. On all sides of me kid campers would be winding up their legs. I wouldn't be able to wind up mine because I would have a dog on them winding up his. Then the monster would speak:

"*Moo.*"

Strange would stop shivering and whining. "Moo?" he would say. "I'm not afraid of anything that says Moo." And at that he would tear out of the sleeping bag and chase the cow off into the night. As soon as he returned, he would walk over and pant his doggy breath into my face. "It's okay now, Boss," he would say. "You go ahead and get some sleep. I'll stand guard."

As I say, kid camping just isn't kid camping unless there's a dog or two along.

Many campgrounds, by the way, have regulations that either prohibit dogs entirely or require that they be kept on a leash. If you and your family are planning a trip to a campground, it's important that you find out in advance what regulations it has pertaining to dogs. Even if there are no regulations, it is simply good camping manners to keep your dog on a leash or by some other means limit his range to your own campsite. You may think of your dog as a lovable and comical fellow but the other campers may not regard him so affectionately, particularly if he persists in charging through their camp in pursuit of squirrels, begging at their dinner table, or leaving his calling card where they want to sleep. There are also people who are terrified of dogs, all dogs, and your friendly, happy mutt will be no more welcome to them than a saber-toothed tiger. Keep him confined to your own camp.

E *Eggs*

When kid campers carry both hard-boiled and raw eggs on a camping trip, parents often wonder how the kids manage to tell the difference between the two. It's easy. The raw eggs are the ones dripping out of the bottom of the pack. This tendency of raw eggs to break inside a pack has resulted in a dish called the Undies Omelet. With this recipe, you wring the eggs out of your spare set of underwear directly into the frying pan. Other variations of this recipe are the Socks Omelet, the Shirt Omelet, and even the Sleeping Bag Omelet.

If these recipes don't sound particularly appetizing to you, perhaps you should equip yourself with a hard plastic container especially designed for carrying raw eggs.

Emergencies

Emergencies are situations where people very often think with their feet, their hands, their elbows—everything but their heads. When an emergency occurs, stop for a moment, collect your thoughts and get them back in your head where they belong. Force yourself to study the situation and decide upon the best action to take. I know people who can take a small difficulty and almost instantly turn it into an emergency. They panic. They jump up and down. They shout and cry. They do everything but what the situation calls for: clear, calm, logical thinking.

Back when I was a kid, the old woodsman Rancid Crabtree and I would occasionally find ourselves in an emergency situation. Now, as soon as I became aware of the emergency, I would immediately go into my routine of rushing about, jumping up and down, shouting, and squeezing prayers into any spaces left between these other activities. While I was occupied in this

OMELET

manner, Rancid would sit down on a log or whatever was handy, stroke his jaw a couple of times, and say, "Wall now, let's jist thank about this fer a minute." His words never failed to calm me, and quite often they even made the emergency disappear.

Real emergencies call for thinking and action, in that order.

Emergency Kit

Never go into the woods without considering the possibility that you may become lost.

On even a short hike, you should carry these items: a jackknife, matches in a waterproof container, an extra sweater or heavy shirt, adhesive bandages, a flashlight, a police whistle, a small mirror, a compass, and a couple of candy bars. (A blast on the whistle will carry much farther in the woods than a shout. The mirror is used to flash a signal at search planes.) It's also a good idea to carry a lightweight waterproof jacket of some kind, and even a plastic sheet that can be used for a shelter. All of this emergency gear will fit neatly into a small day pack with plenty of room to spare. You'll scarcely know it's there until you need it.

F Farms and Farmers

Farms make great places for kid camping. Probably 90 percent of my early kid camping was done on farms. If we happened to forget an important item, we could usually borrow it from the farmer or his wife. "Mrs. Jones," we would say to the farmer's wife, "we wonder if you could loan us some salt and a cup of sugar and a few of those hot cinnamon rolls." Sometimes we had to accept substitutes of apple pie or chocolate cake for the cinnamon rolls, but that was all right with us and we never complained.

You must always ask the farmer for permission to camp on his property. Find out what his rules are and obey them. Otherwise, he probably won't let you camp there again. As always, you want to clean up your campsite so well that it's almost impossible to tell that you ever camped there at all. Farmers become angry, and rightfully so, when people who use their property leave it looking like a garbage dump. Also, try not to bug the farmer any more than is necessary. He has work to do and doesn't have any time to be bugged.

Treat your farmer right and he will treat you right.

In all my life so far, the finest campsite I've ever had was on a neighbor's farm where two streams came together in a wood of pine, larch, birch, cedar, and fir. The streams contained cutthroat, rainbow, and eastern brook trout, most of which were only slightly smarter than we were. Beavers had built a nice series of dams on one of the streams, construction that the farmer wasn't particularly happy about, but which we kid campers highly favored. The backwater from the dams made a pleasant swamp for us to explore and generally fool about in. There were deer and even bear in the woods, along with the usual squirrels, chipmunks, rabbits, grouse, and a few hundred other kinds of wildlife. And it was all ours because most adult campers would never even think about camping on a farm.

If there are farms near your home, check them out and you'll find some great places to camp.

Feet

Feet are odd-shaped things that are found at the ends of campers' legs and are used for transportation. Wise campers and hikers take good care of their feet, sprinkling them with foot powder, putting dry, clean socks on them twice a day, and babying them along in general. Whenever campers try on a new pair of hiking shoes or boots, they always ask their toes and heels, "You guys got plenty of room in there?" If the toes and heels don't reply, "Yeah, Boss, feels good in here!" the campers find more comfortable quarters for their feet. Allowing their feet to get blisters is the worst thing campers and hikers can do to their feet (see Blisters), unless there happens to be an ax along. Axes can do terrible things to feet.

Take care of your feet and they will take care of you. Never let your feet do your thinking for you, however. They are not much good at it (see Directions).

First Aid

Everyone should know the basics of first aid, and hikers and campers perhaps more than others. The YMCA, YWCA, the Red Cross, the Boy Scouts and Girl Scouts all offer instruction in first aid. Since many first aid techniques are best learned through demonstration and supervised practice, you should try to enroll in such a course. The Boy Scout *Fieldbook* has a good section on safety and first aid. *The First Aid Textbook*, published by the American National Red Cross, can be purchased through your local Red Cross chapter.

Flashlights

Anyone who plans to spend a day hiking in the woods should carry a flashlight because days have a way of turning into nights before they are expected to. A flashlight is an essential item for any hike that has the slightest chance of turning into an overnight trip.

Alkaline batteries, size C or D depending on your flashlight, will allow you to keep your flashlight on all night without having its light fade out. Standard batteries last for only an hour or two.

At night, your flashlight should be kept within easy reach and in a place where you won't have trouble finding it in the dark. A side pocket on your pack is a good place. You can also tie a cord to your flashlight and hang the cord from a branch or tent pole.

Fly Sheet

The fly sheet is a rectangle of canvas, plastic, or nylon with ties or grommets around the edges. It is rigged up over a tent to keep rain off of it. It can also be used as a shelter by itself (see Tents). Fly sheets are often put up over picnic tables in campgrounds so the campers can eat outside but still be protected from sun and rain. On a backpacking trip, it's a good idea to have two fly sheets along. One is used over the tent or as a shelter itself. The other one is rigged up to provide shelter for working, sitting, eating, and keeping camp gear from getting soaked.

Foam Pad

Many campers prefer foam pads to air mattresses, even though they can't float down a creek on a foam pad. Foam pads are bulky to carry but you don't have to blow them up or squeeze air out of them. They also give better insulation from ground cold than air mattresses do, and they don't puncture. Foam pads come in three-quarter and full-length sizes. Many kinds of foam pads are sold in camping departments, and almost all of them work fine for kid camping. The better ones are about 2 inches thick and are covered on the bottom with waterproof nylon and on top with cotton or other non-slick fabric, which the camper is less likely to slip off of.

Foraging

It is still possible to forage for wild foods, but you need to be taught firsthand by experts how to recognize what wild plants and fungi are edible, inedible, or downright poisonous. But make sure the person who is teaching you is actually an expert. Once I had a fellow break off a few leaves from a plant and tell me, "Here, try this. It's miner's lettuce." We both took a leaf and chewed on it for a second or two. Then the fellow said, "Hmmmmm. Maybe this ain't—*gag*—miner's lettuce after all!" So I replied, "I—*gag*—would have to agree with you—*gag, gag*—about that." As it turned out, the plant, whatever it was, was not poisonous but it certainly could have fooled me at the time. For one thing, it made me extremely tired, possibly because I had to run nearly a mile to get a drink of water to wash the taste out of my mouth.

Many edible wild plants are also regarded as weeds by farmers, the forest service, the highway department and others. Or they may be growing in the company of weeds. In any case, weeds are often sprayed with poisons, and this is another reason to be doubly careful when foraging for wild foods, if you risk doing it at all.

Most kid campers do their foraging in their mother's kitchen, refrigerator, and pantry. This is called "living off the land" by kid campers. It is called something else by mothers.

Forked Sticks

One would think forked sticks would be in great abundance in the world, but you can never seem to find them when you want them. When you do find them they're usually part of a live tree. I for one don't favor cutting down a 30-foot tree in order to get a 2-foot forked stick.

What you use forked sticks for is to hold up your cooking spit over a fire. A forked stick is pounded into the ground on each side of your fireplace—I am here skipping over the difficulty of pounding a forked stick—and the stick used for the cooking spit is laid in the notches. Actually, it is much simpler to use straight sticks for uprights and tie the crosspiece to them. The only reason that forked sticks became popular must be that back in the old days they didn't have twine or wire. Once again, I think the proper practice in the woods nowadays is to avoid cutting anything that doesn't have to be cut, and forked sticks certainly are not essential to the camper.

Forked sticks come in handy for supporting crosspieces whenever you don't have other means of fastening them to upright poles. If no forked sticks are available, you might try the dovetail-notch method of fastening two pieces of wood together. The Boy Scout *Fieldbook* contains illustrated, step-by-step directions for the dove-tail notch.

Freeze-dried

Freeze-dried foods are lightweight, won't spoil, and generally are delicious, at least compared to most camp food. A freeze-dried hamburger patty looks and feels like a dried-up sponge. Soak it in a pan of water, though, and the sponge plumps up into your regular juicy burger ready for cooking.

Freeze-dried foods you can buy include beefsteaks, porkchops, ham slices, precooked bacon, scrambled eggs, meatballs, shrimp, hash, chicken with rice, chili with beans, potatoes, corn, peas, peaches, fruit cocktail, and even strawberries. (The strawberries I've tried have been terrible, but a camper can't expect everything.)

Freeze-dried foods can be bought in most camping supplies departments and stores. They come in foil bags that contain servings ranging from 1 to 4. The one drawback to freeze-dried foods is that they are expensive.

I have often wondered why a backpack couldn't be freeze-dried. You could carry it in your pocket to the campsite, soak it in a creek for a few minutes, and your whole camp would plump up right before your eyes. One of these days some manufacturer will probably steal my idea and start turning out complete freeze-dried camps.

Frogs

Frogs often show up in the strangest places on kid camping trips. It is not unusual for them to find their way into sleeping bags, pockets, and hats. I don't know why frogs do this unless they like to hear people going *Aaaaiii!*

G   *Gasp*

Upon returning from a camping trip, you should never allow your mother to open your pack and look inside, because she will probably gasp. Gasping directly over a kid's open pack immediately after a camping trip can cause a mother's face to turn green. And nobody wants a mother with a green face, except possibly a Martian.

Girl Scouts

Camping and hiking programs for Girl Scouts start at age six, and there is probably no better way for girls to learn camping techniques than by joining this excellent organization. The Girl Scouts do three kinds of camping—day camping, where you spend the day out and go home at night; resident camping, where you stay out for a week or more, living in tents or cabins with girls your own age; and troop camping, where you go out with your troop for as long as you want. In troop camping, girls learn about hiking, tying knots, building fires, and cooking over fires. They also learn about the stars and the weather, and how to use a map and compass. They study outdoor survival skills and learn how to make much of their own camping equipment. The only bad thing about the Girl Scouts is that boys aren't allowed to join.

Glasses

Campers who wear glasses always must face the problem of where to put them during the night so that they won't

GASP

get lost or stepped on. Just recently my friend Retch and I were sleeping in a small backpacking tent and Retch got up to make one of his frequent trips to the outside.

"Watch out!" I yelled at him. "You're stepping on my glasses!"

"I'm sorry," he said. "I thought you still had them on."

"I do!" I yelled.

I mention this only by way of showing that almost no place is safe for your glasses if you are sleeping in a tent with one or more individuals who insist upon getting up and roaming around at night. I usually put my specs into their case and then stick the case into one of my boots.

Gorp

Every camping trip requires a good supply of gorp. Take a plastic bag and toss in a mixture of sugar-coated chocolates, candy orange slices, pretzels, cheese crackers, salted peanuts, dried fruit, whatever you like, and you have gorp. Gorp is sort of a movable snack, providing campers with quick energy on the trail. These days, gorp has pretty much been displaced by granola.

Here is one recipe for granola. You can make your own variations of it.

GRANOLA

2½ cups instant oatmeal
½ cup sunflower seeds
½ cup sesame seeds
½ cup wheat germ
½ cup chopped nuts
½ cup shredded coconut
½ cup soybeans

½ cup powdered milk
½ cup brown sugar
½ cup honey
½ cup vegetable oil

Put all the ingredients except the honey and vegetable oil into a large bowl and stir and mix. Combine the honey and oil and pour over the dry ingredients. Mix well.

Spread the mixture in a large shallow pan with sides and bake in the oven at 250° (low heat) until it is golden brown. (Stir it occasionally to toast evenly.) Remove from oven and cool.

Grit

When I was a boy, I would often accompany the old woodsman Rancid Crabtree to inspect his trap line in the middle of the winter. When I would complain about being wet and cold and tired and hungry, he would tell me, "What you need, boy, is more grit." I thought it was something to eat. It isn't. You can't buy grit; you have to earn it. One of the best places to earn it is on kid camping trips. Each camping trip gives you a bit more grit. Eventually, you will have a good supply of grit, and it will serve you well all your life. I can't tell you exactly what grit is, but you'll know it when you get it. Grit is one of the great side benefits of camping.

I remember once in seventh grade some friends and I were planning a camping trip just after the snow had gone off in early spring. We invited another kid to go along with us, but he scoffed in our faces. It was bad enough to have our faces scoffed in, but then he went up to our scoutmaster and said, "Do you know what those crazy guys want me to do? They want me to go camping with them in this miserable weather!" Naturally, we were embarrassed. Then the scoutmaster said, "Maybe you should accept the invitation, Felix. It would give you some grit." That, of course, made us feel pretty good. Felix didn't go on the camping trip anyway, but if he had, he certainly would have picked up some grit. That was about the grittiest camping trip I've ever been on.

Groundsheet

This is a waterproof sheet that you place on the ground under your bedroll or sleeping bag. It prevents ground moisture from seeping up into your bed and keeps your bed out of the dirt. It also helps protect your air mattress if you are using one. A cheap sheet of plastic works fine as a groundsheet. If you're using a bedroll, the groundsheet should be wide enough to fold over the top of your blankets to keep them from getting damp. Your bedroll should be rolled up in the groundsheet when you are carrying it on the outside of your pack. If your bedroll is inside your pack, you can use the groundsheet to cover your pack and yourself while hiking in the rain.

H Hash

This is what most camp meals appear to be even though they are actually something else, such as scrambled eggs, hash brown potatoes, or spaghetti and tomato sauce. Campers distinguish between these dishes by calling them Yellow Hash, Brown Hash, and Red Hash.

"Heroes"

One of the worst pests to be found on camping trips is a "hero." A "hero" is the person who always has to be first and best.

Here is how to recognize a "hero": He or she will be the individual who crowds past the other hikers on the trail in order to be "the leader." If there are two heroes in the group, they will practically race each other up the trail.

A hero will think he or she is the only one who knows how to set up the tent or build the fire or which direction to take.

Heroes often tempt other campers into taking unnecessary risks. "Don't be chicken," they will say. "C'mon, let's climb up the rock slide. We'll get to the top of the mountain quicker that way." Heroes are not only boring, they are dangerous.

Hunkering

Hunkering is one of the most useful of all postures for camping. It is a form of sitting where you use yourself as a chair. Here's how to hunker. Bend your knees and ease yourself down until your rear is resting on the backs of your legs just above the heels. Rest your arms on your knees for balance. That's all there is to it.

It is quite a bit easier for kids to hunker than it is for grown-ups. Actually, it's not difficult for adults to get into a hunker, just for them to get out of it. Occasionally, you will see an adult camper waddle by with his knees up near his ears. This will be a camper who is looking for a tree trunk that he can use to pull himself up out of his hunker. Not everyone can look at a moving hunker without laughing, but try not to do so within hearing of the hunkered camper.

Even for kids, it is best to avoid hunkering while wearing a

"HERO"

full pack. There is no more terrible spectacle to witness than a camper with a full pack trying to get up out of a hunker. The noises he makes are rude and ghastly, and the expression on his face can give you nightmares.

Hypothermia

This is one of the most dangerous things that can happen to a camper. It means that the body is losing its heat. Hypothermia can occur not only in the cold of winter but even on a summer day when a camper is wet and cold for too long. This is why it is important for the camper to carry proper clothes for protection against rain, wind, and cold at all times. (See Clothes.) It is especially important to keep the head and neck warm because as much as fifty percent of the body's heat loss can occur there.

Should a situation come up where you or one of your companions is injured, it is very important that the injured person be kept warm and sheltered while help is being obtained. He or she can be covered with sleeping bags or extra clothing and a rain fly. (See Emergency Kit.) If the person who is injured still shows sign of being chilled, one or two of the other campers should lie next to the camper so that their body heat will keep him or her warm.

Insect Repellent

It is possible to get by without insect repellent on camping trips if you don't mind going home with little red bumps all over your face, neck, arms, and hands. I always carry a bottle of insect repellent with me whenever I head for the woods. "Off" is one I know that works.

J Jitters

Campers sometimes get the jitters. Strangely, nobody ever seems to get just one jitter. Probably one jitter isn't worth mentioning. Jitters often come by the case. You'll hear somebody say, "I've just got a bad case of the jitters." Campers seldom seem to get a *good* case of the jitters, although I suppose it's possible. I've never seen a jitter myself nor have I ever talked to anybody who has seen one, so I don't know what one looks like. My sister used to complain that something gave her "the creeps." I can tell you right now that if I'm out camping, I'd ten times rather get the jitters than the creeps. Jitters sound downright comforting compared to the creeps.

K Knives

A good pocketknife is the camper's most useful tool. The official Boy Scout knife is about right. It has a large blade, a can opener, a bottle opener, a punch, and a screwdriver. The Swiss army knife is also good, but avoid the models with more than six or seven tools—they're too heavy. My own pocketknife has a tiny pair of scissors on it, and I have found this accessory almost as useful as the blade.

You should also have a small sharpening stone to touch up the blade of your knife from time to time. The stone will have a rough side and a fine side. Stroke the blade on the rough side until it starts to be sharp. Then finish it off on the fine side of the stone. Sharpening stones come with illustrated directions for their proper use.

If you carry a sheath knife, make sure it is worn well back on your hip and behind a belt loop so it can't slip forward. A sharp knife can be driven right through a leather sheath and into your upper thigh if it's worn too far forward and you happen to have a bad fall.

L   *Lightning*

Lightning can be scary, no doubt about it. If you use some routine precautions, however, the danger of your being struck by it is slight. The first thing to remember is to stay out from under tall trees, particularly trees that stand alone in an open space, such as in the middle of a pasture. Lightning is attracted to these trees and the electrical charge will be carried down the trunk to where you are standing. Stay away from wire fences, because if the fence is hit even at considerable distance from you, the charge will travel down the wire. Don't stand in a brushy area either, because a close lightning strike will send the charge crackling through the brush, especially if the brush is wet from rain. Stay out of open spaces. If you are up on a mountain ridge when the storm comes up, move well down off the ridge; lightning will almost always strike the mountain peak first and then "walk" down the ridge that runs in the direction the storm is moving.

My own choice for a place to be during a lightning storm is just about anywhere not mentioned above. Usually, I'll just hunker down on the trail and pull a poncho or rain fly over me to keep off the rain.

Some packs are fastened to metal frames. Since metal attracts lightning, it's a good idea to shuck off the pack and stash it some distance from you until the storm has passed over.

Once you have taken the necessary precautions, sit back and

enjoy the storm; lightning can put on a display of fireworks that makes the average Fourth of July celebration look like a convention of fireflies.

Line

Buy a 50-foot roll of ¼-inch nylon rope. This is twice as much as an adult camper needs and is nearly enough for a kid camper. It will have no end of uses. The rope will be cut and tied back together many times over the course of a summer's camping, but remember to tape the cut ends or else hold them over a flame to melt so that they won't unravel.

Litter

The backpacker's motto is "Pack it in, pack it out." If you're a really good camper, you not only pack out what you've packed in, you also pack out what other people have packed in and left in campsites and along trails. In recent years, my backpacking friends and I have taken to carrying an extra plastic bag just to carry out found garbage. This is a common practice among many backpackers nowadays. You might feel a bit disgusted about having to clean up after a bunch of jerks to whom the whole world is a garbage can. On the other hand, you'll feel better for having picked up their litter.

The worst litter is the aluminum pull-tabs off beverage cans. Not only will they last forever as an offense to the eyes of any true camper, but also pull-tabs can give you a nasty gash if stepped on with a bare foot. Last summer three other campers and I spent nearly an hour picking up pull-tabs that had accumulated in and around a campsite near a mountain lake. From the air, that campsite must have sparkled in the sun as if it were covered with sequins.

Aluminum foil, glass bottles, and anything made of plastic are particularly bad forms of litter because they don't decompose. But even a paper gum wrapper tossed carelessly onto a trail detracts from the beauty of an area more than you might think. Most true campers would as soon confront a grizzly bear on the trail as one gum wrapper.

Remember, it is better to pick up the litter than to curse the litterer, but it's all right with me if you do both.

Logs

One of the dangers in the woods that one seldom hears about is logs. Be careful about stepping on them and even more careful about walking on them. For one thing, they can roll on you, and you really haven't been rolled on until you've been rolled on by a log. (Look at a pizza and you'll get the picture of the result.) The more common danger with logs, however, is this: When a tree falls, many of its branches are snapped off, leaving wood spikes as sharp and deadly as daggers sticking up from the trunk. If you are walking a log and your feet slip out from under you and you land sitting down—well, you get the idea. Loggers, who work in the woods all their lives, fear these jagged ends of branches more than almost anything else.

Sometimes trees don't fall all the way to the ground but get hung up in other trees. Never walk under these hung-up trees, of course, and avoid being on the downhill side of them. Trees die standing up, too, in which case they are called snags. The tops of snags, particularly when it is windy, will break off and come crashing to the ground. Stay clear of snags, and never, never chop on them for firewood.

J M *Maps*

Sooner or later every serious camper falls in love with maps, so you might as well get acquainted with them as soon as possible. The best maps for campers and hikers are the topographical ones, which, once you know how to read them, will tell you much about the kind of terrain you will be hiking over. A regular map will show that a section of trail you plan to hike is six miles long, but a topographical map will also show that the section of trail goes over a 3000-foot-high mountain. You now know that the hike will take about three times longer than expected.

To get one of these maps, send a postcard to Map Information Office, U.S. Geological Survey, General Services Building, 18th and F Streets, N.W., Washington D.C. 20405, and request a free *Topographical Map Index Circular* of the state or states in which you plan to do your hiking and a free folder describing topographical maps. The index circular contains a small map of the state divided into sections called "quadrangles." There is a separate map for each quadrangle. Figure out which quadrangles your expedition will take place in. Then order the maps for those quadrangles. For areas east of the Mississippi River, order the maps from the Geological Survey in Washington; for areas west of the Mississippi, order the maps from U.S. Geological Survey, Federal Center, Denver, Colorado 80200. Send proper payment for the maps. In larger cities, you may be able to obtain the topographical maps at your regional Geological Survey Office. Topographical maps are also sold in sporting goods stores.

The "Map and Compass" chapter of the *Fieldbook* of the Boy Scouts of America is a good place to start your study of maps.

Marshmallows

Until the invention of marshmallows, all there was for campers to do around the campfire in the evening was to stare into the flames. The marshmallow revolutionized camping. Not only did it provide campers with a delicious after dinner snack, it created a whole new sport—marshmallow toasting.

The object of the sport of marshmallow toasting is to twirl the toasting stick over the fire in such a manner that the marshmallow turns a golden brown all over without bursting into flames. The person who toasts the most marshmallows in this manner is the winner. Since it is required that each participant eat all the marshmallows he or she toasts, the winners and runners-up are easily recognized by their green hue and bloated cheeks.

There are several different ways of eating toasted marshmallows, but the most enjoyable is to suck out the melted interior, leaving an empty "skin," which is popped into the mouth at the end of the process. Mothers often describe this method as "too gross for words." What better recommendation could you want?

Matches

If it is possible for matches to get wet, they will. A friend of mine stuck a couple of books of matches in a shirt pocket under his waterproof parka so that they would be protected from the rain. The matches became soaked—not from the rain, but from his own perspiration. He finally managed to get a fire started by resorting to a tried-and-true method I myself had taught him: he borrowed some dry matches from his hiking companion.

Matches should always be carried in a waterproof container.

Plastic aspirin bottles with snap-on, moistureproof caps work fine. You can also purchase matchsafes, special containers designed for campers to carry their matches in. Dipping the tips of matches in melted paraffin will make them waterproof. Or you can buy waterproof matches.

Don't carry wooden matches loose in your pocket. I once saw a kid in high school have several matches in his pocket accidentally ignite. At first, I didn't know what had happened—I thought he had invented some wild new dance. As it turned out, he was not badly burned, but even so he was not eager to repeat the performance.

There are devices called "metal matches," which, when scraped or struck with a piece of metal, throw off a shower of sparks. The idea is to direct the sparks into dry tinder and in that way get your fire started.

Moleskin

Hikers dumb enough to get blisters should at least be smart enough to carry moleskin with them to make patches to cover the blisters. How do you make a moleskin patch? Well, first you catch a mole . . . No, only kidding about that. Moleskin is a thin sheet of felt with adhesive on one side. You can can buy it in drugstores. (See Blisters for uses of moleskin.)

Moseying

This is one of the best paces for the kid camper. The hiker who moseys along will feel more, enjoy more, and see more than a whole herd of campers who go down the trail as if

MOSEYING

they were participating in a stampede. All of the great woodsmen and woodswomen that I have ever known were experts at the art of moseying.

Here's how to mosey. Take two or three easy steps. Then stop and look around. Turn over a rock with the toe of your boot and see what's under it. Take a half dozen more easy steps, and look around again. Hitch up your pants. Now stroll for fifty yards or so, stop, take another casual look around, maybe rest your pack on a rock or log, eat a handful of gorp, snap a couple of pictures of wildflowers, and then continue on up the trail at an easy pace for a hundred yards or so, where you stop again and repeat the whole process. About this time you will have caught up with one or more of the speedy hikers who shot past you a while before on the trail. Be careful not to step on their tongues as you mosey past them.

Mosquitoes

Campers like to tell lies about the size and ferocity of mosquitoes encountered on their outings. My friend Retch, for example, tells about the time he was attacked by a swarm of mosquitoes so huge they lifted him clear off the road. He says they probably would have gotten away with him, too, if he hadn't been in his car. Now I know that's a lie. I've seen a lot of mosquitoes in my time, and not more than a couple hundred of them were big enough to carry off anything heavier than a dog and only a medium-size dog at that. Take my word for it, and don't believe any of the tall tales you hear about mosquitoes. Some campers just can't resist telling lies about them.

Mosquitoes can be a nuisance and even a misery in just their ordinary size and numbers. People are a mosquito's idea of a giant strawberry soda. A good mosquito repellent, such as Off, will usually keep them from dipping their straws into you. Even so, you can be driven almost batty by clouds of them hovering about your head, particularly when you're trying to sleep. This is one reason campers often carry a bug-proof tent.

Mosquitoes and flies are the only reason for setting up your camp in an area open to the wind rather than in a sheltered spot. The breeze will keep most of the mosquitoes and flies away from you and the others will have to work so hard fighting the breeze, they'll be too tired to cause you much trouble.

You may have heard that smearing mud all over your face, neck, and arms will keep mosquitoes from dining on you. The only reason this might work is that the mosquitoes would be laughing so hard they wouldn't be able to get their straw to go in.

A heavy shirt or sweater with long sleeves will protect most of your top part from mosquitoes. Since mosquitoes tend to come out in the cool part of the day, you'll probably want to wear a heavy shirt or sweater anyway. A bandana will protect your neck and prevent mosquitoes from getting inside your shirt.

Mountain Sickness

Hiking too fast, too far, and too soon at high elevations will often bring on an illness called mountain sickness. Symptoms include headache, dizziness, and nausea. To avoid this misery, take it easy the first couple of days you are in the mountains, and give your body a chance to adjust to the higher elevation. Practice your moseying (see Moseying).

N Never

This is the only time it's all right to leave your campsite in a mess, to dump your garbage in a creek, to panic when lost, to chop down live trees, to leave campfires unattended, to ignore sore places on your feet while hiking, to hike or camp alone, to be a "hero," or to do any of the other things good campers and hikers know are dumb. All the rest of the time, of course, these practices should be avoided.

Nincompoop

This is a kind of camper that seems to be on the increase. The nincompoop camper considers the whole world to be his own personal garbage can. As of now, no one has developed a cure for nincompoopism, at least none that is legal.

O Oops!

This is one of the worst things a camp cook can say. A camp cook can say "Oops!" under his or her breath and the other campers will hear it twenty yards away.

"Why did you say 'Oops!'?" they will ask.

"No reason," the camp cook will say, smiling evilly. "Every once in a while I just like to say 'Oops!'"

Nobody believes this, of course. A person doesn't say "Oops!" for no reason. As a result, the other campers examine each bite they take of the meal with great suspicion.

The only time campers pay no attention when the camp cook says "Oops!" is when there isn't much of the chocolate pudding

being prepared. Under these circumstances, he or she may shout out "Oops!" four or five times, and no one will even seem to notice.

ℙ Packs

The three most common kinds of packs are day packs, frame rucksacks, and frame packs.

The day pack, as the name suggests, is used for day hikes. It is small, usually made of nylon, and has some snap rings and small straps on it for carrying items you don't want to stick inside. Use it for carrying your emergency kit, lunch, camera, extra sweater, etc.

The frame rucksack is, to my mind, ideal for the kid camper. It is small enough to use as a day pack but large enough to carry all the stuff you'll need for a camping trip lasting a night or two. Rucksacks are very comfortable to carry.

Frame packs are often referred to as backpacks. They consist of a tubular aluminum frame to which the pack is fastened. They are best for long trips, where you need to carry a great deal of supplies and gear. Compartments and numerous large outside pockets help you to keep your stuff organized.

A waist belt will help relieve the weight on your shoulders when you are carrying a heavy pack. It is attached to the bottom of your pack frame and buckles around your waist, so that much of the weight of the pack is centered over your legs. The idea is to divide the weight between your legs and your shoulders. To rest your shoulders, you need only to straighten up and let your legs take the full weight of the pack. Most waist belts are padded to make them more comfortable.

Packing the pack. Some experts say that the pack should be loaded so that the most weight is at the top. Others say the most weight should be at the bottom. And still others say that it doesn't make any difference. I like the weight to be in the bottom of the pack myself, because it seems to improve my balance.

Some backpacks have a three-quarter-length pack on the frame; the bottom quarter of the frame is left vacant for strapping on a sleeping bag. That puts the lightest item at the bottom of the pack. If you have a choice, I suggest you get a full-length pack and then the sleeping bag can be placed inside it, at the top or bottom, whichever you prefer. In any case, if it's inside the pack it will be much less likely to get wet.

Heavy objects, such as food sacks, should be placed as close to your back as possible. If the heavy objects are loaded away from your back, they will put more strain on your shoulders and make it more difficult to keep your balance.

Items that you may need from time to time during the hike, such as camera, snack bag, and extra clothes, should be placed at the top of the pack so that you don't have to unload everything whenever you want to snack, take a picture, or put on a sweater.

Food items should be put in a strong plastic bag, preferably a double bag. This will keep your food stores organized in the pack and the bag can also be used to hang your food out of reach of bears at night if you happen to be in bear country (see Bears).

Toilet gear kit, emergency kit, cook kit, dirty clothes, and garbage should all have their own separate bags.

Putting a pack on and taking it off is a bit of an art. If possible, set the pack up on a bank, a stump, the tailgate of a station wagon, or whatever is handy and then slip into the shoulder straps. To take the pack off, reverse the procedure. Otherwise, just wrestle it on and wrestle it off. After a while you will find a method you prefer.

Pedometer

This little instrument measures how far you walk. About the size of a pocket watch, it attaches to your belt and must be adjusted to the length of your particular stride. The problem with having a pedometer along is that when you are certain you must have walked at least fifteen miles, it will indicate that you've actually walked only two miles.

Planning

Many camping experts will tell you that careful planning is essential to a successful camping trip. This is true of other camping but not of kid camping. I recall many fine camping trips as a youngster in which my friends and I did absolutely no planning at all except to agree, more or less, on the time for leaving and returning, and the destination. When we arrived at our campsite, we would then ask each person what food he had brought so we could prepare the supper menu.

"I brought potatoes and onions," Norm would say. "What did you bring, Pat?"

"Some potatoes and onions. What did you bring, Vern?"

"I just hope you guys like potatoes and onions as much as I do," Vern would say. "For supper we can have fried fish and potatoes and onions, if we catch some fish."

This lack of planning prevented many arguments about what to have for supper.

Planning, I should point out, is not against the rules of kid camping. Some kids find that it is fun and can even improve the quality of the trip in many ways.

Pockets

Pockets are very important to campers. Make sure you have plenty of pockets in your shirt, pants, and jacket or parka. What the average camper does during the course of a trip is to transfer most of the contents of the pack to his or her pockets. It is this practice that causes campers to appear lumpy and bulgy.

Q Quack

If you are camped near water, you may be awakened very early in the morning by a single, loud *quack*. This is the signal given by a sentry duck to tell all the other ducks in the flock that a new day has begun. It is called "the quack of dawn." Perhaps you've heard of it.

Queasy

When sleeping in a two-person tent with someone, you will often hear that individual say he or she "feels" something: "I feel a rock under my back. . . . I feel a crawly thing. . . . Boy, do I feel tired. . . . I feel like a hamburger and a strawberry shake." You can safely ignore all of these feelings, because they don't involve you directly. However, if the individual says, "Gee, my stomach feels really queasy!" then that is cause for alarm. A two-person tent is no place to be with a person whose stomach feels really queasy. Suggest that your partner step outside for a breath of fresh air. If she or he refuses to act upon this suggestion, you should consider stepping outside for a breath of fresh air yourself. It will make you feel better.

Quickly

This is how you go back down the trail to get your father's binoculars after he finds out you left them at the last rest stop.

R Roamers of the Night

For some unknown reason, certain campers can never hear the call of nature until after everyone has settled down for the night. Let's say that you're sleeping out with a few friends on a pitch-dark night. Almost everyone has finally drifted into a sound sleep; then, suddenly, comes the sound of a sleeping bag being unzipped. Instantly, every camper is awake. A Roamer of the Night is up! He or she has heard the call of nature. Nature called everybody else three hours ago but this individual didn't hear. The Roamer's footsteps wander this way, then that way. "Ooooh! Ahh!" somebody yells. "Get off! You're standing on my stomach!" A stack of kettles goes crashing into the dirt. Then the Roamer falls on top of another camper and there are grunting and thumping sounds. The dog wakes up and starts barking. Cows in the nearby pasture stampede, mooing and bellowing. The ruckus goes on until finally the Roamer gets his or her business tended to and is once again back in bed. Silence. Sleep. Then comes the sound of the next sleeping bag zipper being run down.

Rocks

Rocks have many uses on camping trips. They can be used to build fireplaces, as weights to secure lines of tents and fly sheets, for sitting on, and for skipping along the surface of water. There are also a couple of things that should not be done with rocks:

Never roll rocks down the side of a mountain; other campers and wildlife may be down below, and your rock might even set off a landslide.

Rocks that have been in or near water should not be used around a campfire, because they might explode when they get hot.

S S-Hooks

S-hooks are used for hanging pots from your cooking spit over the fire. You can purchase them in some camping supplies stores but they are easy to make. The wire you use to make them needs to be heavy enough that the weight of the pots and their contents won't straighten out the S and dump your supper in the fire. When I made my S-hooks, I happened to find a wire in my garage of about the same diameter as a pencil. It worked fine. However, if you have to go out and buy just the right gauge of wire, (1) you will probably have trouble finding some, and (2) it would be cheaper and simpler and easier just to buy the S-hooks. My research shows, on the other hand, that almost every family in the United States has at least four dozen wire coat hangers more than they have clothes to hang on them. Your parents should be happy to give you all you want.

With a pair of wire cutters, snip off the wire on each side of the place where it is twisted together. Straighten this length of wire and cut it in two in the middle. Bend half a loop in one end of the wire and another half hook in the other end so that the wire forms a skinny S. Bend the middle of the wire so that the bottom hook is directly under the top hook; this will allow the hook to hang straight down from the cooking spit. The size of the top hook can be rebent in camp to fit the diameter of your cooking spit if need be. My experiments show that an S-hook made from a wire coat hanger is strong enough to hold a cooking kettle, filled slightly more than half full, of approximately the size of a 1-pound coffee can or any of the kettles in a backpacker's cook kit. If stronger S-hooks are needed, simply twist together the wires of two coat hangers for double the strength. Two S-hooks 6 inches long and two 10 inches long should be adequate for any camp. Keep in mind that the long S-hooks can be made shorter simply by bending the hooks closer to each other. The cut ends of coat hanger wire are sharp. Take a pair of pliers and bend the very end of each wire back over so that the tips are rounded.

Sleeping Bags (also see Bedroll)

My first sleeping bag was purchased at an army surplus store and consisted of a wool blanket sewn into the general shape of a mummy and was in fact called "a mummy bag." Possibly, a mummy would have been comfortable in it but I wasn't. After a few camping trips on which I entertained my companions by turning blue and setting a record for teeth-chattering, I bought another army surplus sleeping bag. The filler in this one, if I'm not mistaken, was chicken feathers. In any case, every time the bag got rained on I went home smelling like a wet chicken. Finally I acquired a good sleeping bag, one that I used for a dozen years and which my kids still use.

Most families nowadays have at least two or three sleeping bags around the house, and kid campers usually have to make do with whatever is available. If you have your choice of a sleeping bag, however, I suggest you get the style referred to as a "mummy bag," a greatly improved version of my first mummy bag. Mummy bags are filled with either down from waterfowl or with artificial insulation. One advantage of the mummy bag is that it can be closed at the top so that only your face is sticking out. Perhaps the best thing about mummy bags is that they can be stuffed into stuff bags quickly and easily. You may be familiar with sleeping bags the size and shape of a bunk bed mattress, which allow cold air to sneak in gaps at the top. These bags come with enough drawstring attached to them to knit a sweater for an elephant. It is impossible to keep the drawstrings untangled. After a hundred times or so, you will figure out how to roll up the bag into a neat, little, compact cylinder and get all the drawstrings to come out just right and will be able to do so without having your mother threaten to wash out your mouth with soap. You will always detest this chore, so as soon as possible get yourself a mummy bag that stuffs into a stuff bag.

When buying a mummy bag, make sure that it is equipped with both snaps and zipper. Zippers have a way of becoming broken, stuck, or otherwise unable to do the job expected of them. When the zipper fails to function, you can close the bag with the snaps. Most sleeping bags are constructed of long tubes filled with insulation. Check to see whether there is plenty of insulation along the seams connecting the tubes to each other. If the bag is properly designed, there will be.

When the bag is pressed tightly into a stuff bag, all of the air gets squeezed out of the filler. It is this air in the filler that keeps the cold from getting inside the bag with the camper. Whenever you are preparing your bed for the night, remember to shake up the bag so that the filler fluffs up and traps new air.

Soap

Use biodegradable soap, which means that it won't gunk up the environment. It comes in a tube and you can use it for washing your clothes, your dishes, and yourself. There are various brands and they can be bought in camping-supplies stores.

Soap made especially for campers is highly concentrated. A small tube will take care of all your washing needs for trips up to a week in length. A tiny dab is all you need for most washing chores. Get one that works in cold water.

T Tent Pegs

Lightweight metal tent pegs can be purchased for about fifteen cents each. They work better than wooden ones.

Tents

Tents are fun and useful, but usually not necessary for kid camping or even most other kinds of camping.

The simplest "tent" is a waterproof tarp, usually made of strong but lightweight plastic. Nylon fly sheets, which are rigged over the tops of regular tents to keep the rain off, make fine shelters, but a plastic tarp will do the job. Fly sheets and many plastic tarps have grommets, or metal rings, in each corner and on the sides to tie ropes to.

If you are using a piece of plastic that doesn't have grommets or loops to fasten your ropes to, here is a good way to attach ropes to the plastic wherever you need them:

Bug tent: This is a lightweight tent used to keep insects away from campers while they sleep. It isn't intended to provide shelter from rain, so a waterproof fly sheet should be stretched above it if you expect rain.

There are dozens of different makes of lightweight backpackers' tents on the market. Even the cheapest of these is probably fine for kid camping, provided that it is equipped with screened

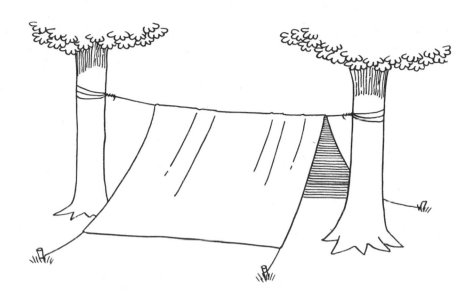

FLYSHEET SHELTER

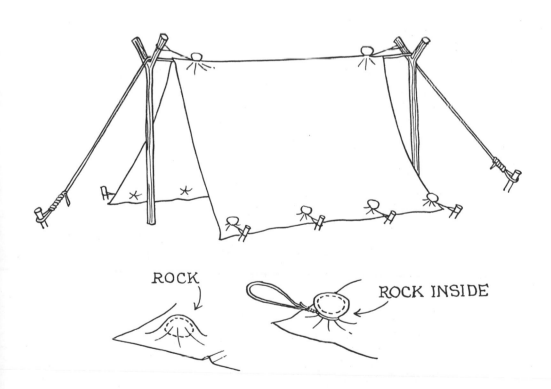

ROCK

ROCK INSIDE

air vents and is otherwise designed to keep out insects. Since one of the main purposes of a tent is to keep out insects, the entrance should be kept closed when not in use; otherwise, your bug tent will become buggy.

Litepack Camping Equipment, pamphlet No. 26-074, a reprint from *Boy's Life* magazine, contains plans for making two different kinds of tents. It can be purchased from your local Boy Scout headquarters for forty cents.

Tin-can Stove

This is a little stove you can make out of a tuna-fish can and a 2-pound coffee can.

Take the lid off the can and eat the tuna fish. If you leave the tuna fish in the can, you're going to have all kinds of trouble. Or you can start with a tuna-fish can that's already empty.

Cut a strip of corrugated cardboard that is just as wide as the can is high. Roll up the cardboard tightly and put it in the can so that the little holes in the cardboard are facing up.

Fill the can with melted paraffin wax. You must get an adult to melt the paraffin for you in a double boiler on the stove, because if the wax gets too hot it will catch fire.

That takes care of the burner. It works like a short, fat candle, with the cardboard serving as a wick.

For the stove, you need an empty 2-pound coffee can. Cut a door on the can as shown in the illustration. Use tin snips for this. Punch holes all the way around the bottom edge of the can as shown. Use one of those can openers that punch triangle-shaped holes.

Light the burner and set the stove over the top of it. You're in business.

You can cook food right on the surface of the stove, but that's

TIN-CAN STOVE

messy and gunks up your stove. It's better to use a foil pan or a regular pan or kettle.

To control the heat of the burner, and to put it out, you need a piece of foil in the shape of the top of the burner and slightly bigger. Fasten this to one end of a length of wire that is bent down at the other end, as shown. Slide the foil partway over the top of the burner to reduce the heat, or all the way over it to snuff out the flame.

The tin-can stove gets very hot. If it happens to get knocked over, resist the urge to grab it with your hands. Hurts!

Trowel

When you are hiking and camping away from campgrounds, you will have to make your own toilet. A trowel or small hand shovel is necessary for this purpose, both for digging the hole and covering it up after use. The site you select for digging your sanitary facility should, of course, be well off the beaten path and away from lakes or streams.

U Urp!

This is the answer campers give to the question, "Anybody want another helping of Whatchamacallit Stew?"

V Very

This is how cold it will be when it's your turn to get up and build the campfire in the morning.

Washing

Many kid campers find this subject dull and would rather skip it, but washing is something that must be done. I remember once in the old days, a kid by the name of Rupert tossed all his dirty dishes and clothes in his packsack at the end of a camping trip and announced, "I'm gonna haul all this stuff home to my mother. Mom does all the washing in our family." Poor old Rupert! On later camping trips, as we were busy washing up our stuff, somebody would occasionally ask, "Gosh, I wonder what ever became of poor old Rupert?"

Washing your face and hands at least once a day is very important on all camping trips. For one thing, it will make you feel like a new person and even look like one. ("Gee, I didn't know that was you," somebody might say.)

A bar of hand soap works fine for washing yourself. Be sure to carry it in its own plastic case or plastic bag or wrapped in foil.

A steel wool scouring pad with the soap in it (Brillo or SOS) should be carried for scrubbing out dirty pans. Soap powder should be carried for dish and clothes washing.

With the exception of the scouring pad, a tube of biodegradable camper's soap will handle *all* washing chores and will not pollute the environment. Many biodegradable soaps work well in cold water.

The most important thing to remember about washing with soap is never to do it in a stream or lake. Always dip up a pot or pail of water and then do your washing at a place well away from the stream or lake. To jump in a lake or stream, soap all up, and then rinse off, is a crime against nature.

Smearing soap around the *outside* of pots and pans before cooking with them over a campfire will make them much easier to clean.

WASHING

Water

Sadly, much of the water found in lakes and streams nowadays is unsafe to drink. To make it safe to drink, drop a couple of halazone tablets into your canteen of water and let stand for thirty minutes. Halazone tablets can be purchased in drugstores or most outdoor sports stores. If you don't like the taste of halazone in the water, you can mix in your favorite flavor of fruit ade. Water can also be made safe to drink by boiling it for ten minutes.

Whistle

Many kids laugh at the idea of carrying a whistle on a camping or hiking trip. They think they can whistle just as loudly through their teeth, which they probably can. But have they ever tried to whistle through chattering teeth? I'll bet not.

If you are lost, a blast on your whistle at frequent intervals will lead searchers to you. A whistle is useful in warning bears of your approach. (See Bears.) Whistle codes can also be invented: two short blasts might mean "Wait for me"; a short and a long, "Come here," and so on.

Whistles like those used by police and referees are the best for campers and hikers. It is not a good idea for hikers in the woods to have cords looped around their necks, so fasten the whistle cord to a buttonhole on your jacket or shirt pocket and carry the whistle in the pocket. Use a large safety pin if you don't have a spare buttonhole.

Wire Coat Hanger

This is a most useful item for kid campers and other campers as well. About the only thing it won't be used for is hanging coats on. It can be shaped into S-hooks for hanging pots from a cooking spit. (See S-hooks.) It also makes a good wiener and marshmallow stick; simply straighten out the hook on the top and squeeze the rest of the coat hanger so that it forms a long handle. When using a coat hanger for a cooking stick, you should always hold it over a flame first to burn off the paint from the section which will hold your food. Wear a glove or use a pot holder to hold the handle because the wire will become hot. Coat hanger cooking sticks are especially useful in campgrounds, some of which have regulations against cutting cooking sticks, and in campgrounds without such regulations all the good wiener sticks will already be cut.

Wire coat hangers will come in handy for almost any situation requiring a stout wire. Be sure to fold back the cut ends of the wire with a pair of pliers so that the tips are rounded; otherwise they will be constantly poking into things you don't want to have poked into. The coat hangers can be folded up for carrying in a pack and straightened out when needed.

X

X

Maps showing where pirate treasure is buried always have the spot marked with an X, right? You never can tell when you might come across one of these X's on one of your camping trips. Along with the litter you've gathered up to pack out, you might carry back a plastic bag full of rubies and diamonds and Spanish doubloons. On the other hand, if there is a pirate standing near the X, forget you ever saw it.

Y

Yipe! Yipe! Yipe!

Bark! Bark! Bark! is the sound your camp dog makes when he is chasing something away from camp. *Yipe! Yipe! Yipe!* is the sound he makes when the something is chasing him back toward camp. Learn to recognize and tell the difference between these two sounds. It will give you a clue as to which direction your dog is moving in and possibly which direction you may want to move in.

Z

Zebras

If you come across a herd of zebras while you are camping, it means that either you have wandered into a zoo or are lost—really lost!

Zip

Two kids are camped out in the backyard on a dark night.

"Did y-you hear a w-weird noise just n-now?" one kid asks.

Zip!

The *Zip* means the other kid heard the weird noise.

About the Author

Patrick F. McManus is well known all over the United States to the readers of *Field & Stream*, of which he is an associate editor. He writes a monthly column for that magazine, and says, "Many of the fan letters I receive come from kids. As a matter of fact, I have also received a number of letters from teachers around the country suggesting that I do some books for children." *Kid Camping from Aaaaiii! to Zip* is his first, although he has written one adult book, *A Fine and Pleasant Misery: Cautionary Tales of the Outdoor Life*.

Born in Sandpoint, Idaho, Mr. McManus lives in Spokane, Washington. He and his wife are the parents of four camping daughters with much experience in Brownies, Blue Birds, Camp Fire Girls, and Girl Scouts. "You wouldn't believe the quantities of four-bean salad I've consumed at father-daughter banquets," he says.

Mr. McManus started his writing career while he was still in college, free-lancing articles to newspapers and national magazines. A college English professor, he is now co-director of the journalism program at Eastern Washington University in Cheney, Washington.